Intercultural Aspects in Teaching English at Primary Schools

Eva Reid

Intercultural Aspects in Teaching English at Primary Schools

PETER LANG
EDITION

Bibliographic Information published by the Deutsche Nationalbibliothek
The Deutsche Nationalbibliothek lists this publication
in the Deutsche Nationalbibliografie; detailed bibliographic
data is available in the internet at http://dnb.d-nb.de.

Library of Congress Cataloging-in-Publication Data

Reid, Eva, 1972-
Intercultural aspects in teaching English at primary schools / Eva
Reid. -- Peter Lang Edition.
   p. cm
Includes bibliographical references.
ISBN 978-3-631-65553-5 -- ISBN 978-3-653-04708-0 (E-Book) 1. English language--Study and teaching (Primary)--Slovakia. 2. English language--Study and teaching (Primary)--Slovak speakers. 3. Intercultural communication--Slovakia. 4. Communication competence in children--Slovakia. 5. Education, Bilingual--Slovakia. I. Title.
PE1068.S54R45 2014
372.652'1094373--dc23
                    2014021261

ISBN 978-3-631-65553-5 (Print)
E-ISBN 978-3-653-04708-0 (E-Book)
DOI 10.3726/978-3-653-04708-0

© Peter Lang GmbH
Internationaler Verlag der Wissenschaften
Frankfurt am Main 2014
All rights reserved.
Peter Lang Edition is an Imprint of Peter Lang GmbH.

Peter Lang – Frankfurt am Main · Bern · Bruxelles · New York ·
Oxford · Warszawa · Wien

This publication has been peer reviewed.

www.peterlang.com

Table of Contents

Introduction

One of the main priorities of the Council of Europe and also Slovak authorities is to equip European citizens with the ability to communicate across linguistic and cultural boundaries in an increasingly multicultural and multilingual Europe, in other words to acquire intercultural communicative competences. Slovakia as a full member of the European Union has an ambition for its citizens to be equally competitive in all fields of science, business, engineering and education with all the other counterparts in the EU. For that reason the Slovak citizens have to be able to communicate professionally in foreign languages and to communicate without any major cultural misunderstandings. Nowadays, Slovak education, including foreign language education, is going through curricular reform. Even though the development of intercultural communicative competences is claimed to be one of the key aims of foreign language teaching, several scholars believe, that most of the teaching time is devoted to the development of the four language skills and that it is often difficult to convince English teachers that the teaching of culture is not a secondary goal. Without doubt culture is an inseparable part of foreign language learning, and this is confirmed by Brooks (2001) who says that language without culture is only a set of symbols which can be misinterpreted, if they are not understood in the right cultural context. Another reason for addressing the issue of acquiring intercultural communicative competences developed from the author's life experiences, which were based on many years of living in three foreign countries and being married to a native English person. Through this personal experience the author became aware of the necessity of being interculturally communicatively competent in order to function successfully during communication using a foreign language with representatives of cultures different to ones own. Ones vested interest and the weight being afforded to this topic by the governing bodies and authorities helped me to make a decision to research the area of teaching intercultural aspects, specifically to find out the reality of the role of culture and intercultural communication in English language education at primary schools in Slovakia.

The study was to provide a holistic overview of the situation starting with the Common European Framework for Languages (2001) its reflection in the national curriculum to the teachers' attitudes and the real teaching of cultural aspects in the

English language lessons. The first part of the monograph offers an insight into the theoretical background of the concept of culture in foreign language education. The role of intercultural teaching within English language lessons is analysed with many scholars' recommendations and tips for methods, techniques and materials. An important part of this chapter is dedicated to the analyses of numerous studies on current research in the area of intercultural communication within ELT. Special attention is paid to three comparable studies (Europublic, 2007; Zerzová, 2012; Kostková, 2012) made independently within different countries. Some of the results can be compared to the current research. The amazing thing is that even though the current research was done qualitatively on a small scale, the results are very similar to the results from the other three studies, which proves the validity of this research. The details of the three studies are dealt with in the first chapter and compared with the current study in the conclusion.

The greatest part of the monograph is dedicated to research methodology and research analyses with conclusions triangulating results of individual research methods. The end of the monograph is dedicated to implications and recommendations for linguo-didactics. In this monograph the mixed qualitative methodology is innovative in the European context and it gets beyond the limitations of the quantitative methods normally used. Three qualitative methods of observation, interview and document analyses with subsequent triangulation were chosen. Different elements of one phenomenon were explored, inter-related and combined into a coherent, convincing and relevant explanation. The aim of the document analyses was to explore and compare the Slovak curricular documents (the pre-reform and current curriculum) with the Common European Framework for Languages (a reference document). As the CEFR does not specify in detail all aspects of cultural learning, I have excerpted and summarised general and communicative competences connected to culture and created clear models. These models were constructed by connecting theories on culture and intercultural communication with cultural contents from CEFR. The proposed models are presented in this monograph and could serve as a base for development of ICC at all levels of English language education. The document analyses show that the current Slovak national curriculum only includes less than a third of the set cultural aspects (based on newly created models from CEFR) which is considered as insufficient. A positive shift can be noticed in the elaboration of sociolinguistic and pragmatic competences, but a negative shift in the area of socio-cultural knowledge. The aim of the observations was to outline the real situation in English language lessons taught at primary schools in Slovakia. The most astonishing finding was that only less than a half of the observed lessons included cultural aspects, even though all the teachers were informed about the aim of the research and were asked to include some cultural teaching into their lessons. English language teachers were interviewed in order to gain additional data considering the implementation of cultural aspects into the English lessons. The findings reveal the fact that most teachers include socio-cultural knowledge (the visible parts of the cultural iceberg) into their lessons and they either neglect or do not realize the importance of the sociolinguistic, pragmatic and paralinguistic aspects (the invisible parts of the cultural iceberg) in the process of acquiring intercultural communicative competences. By triangulation – comparing data from the three research methods – I identified connections, but also contradictions. It can be concluded that many teachers do not know what cultural aspects comprise of and do not understand the importance of acquiring intercultural communicative competences. Most teachers rely on the curriculum as the main guidance for their teaching. If the curriculum does not offer well elaborated guidelines concerning all the important elements of teaching the language, teachers cannot be expected to know how to conduct excellent lessons including all aspects of the language.

The ambition of this monograph is to serve as a valuable source of materials and also as an inspiration for further research.

1. A Statement of the Problem

The research problem that the monograph addresses is the topic of intercultural communication, as it is becoming more and more valid in today's world. Intercultural communicative competence is most often connected with the ability to communicate in a foreign language, but intercultural competence is not necessarily dependant on knowledge of the foreign language. However, paradoxically learning a foreign language should be complemented with learning cultural contents in order to acquire intercultural communicative competence. This is the reason why the current research concentrates on acquiring intercultural competences within English language teaching. Slovak education, including foreign language education in Slovakia, is going through curricular reform. The Slovak curricular documents for foreign language teaching are based on the Common European Framework for Languages: Learning, Teaching, Assessment (CEFR, 2001) and one of the main priorities of the CEFR is to equip pupils with the ability to communicate appropriately with across linguistic and cultural boundaries in multicultural and multilingual Europe. The CEFR was chosen as the reference document for the comparative analyses with the Slovak curricular documents. In this project I want to concentrate on how cultural content is implemented within English language teaching within primary education. The A1 level was chosen according to the CEFR, which represents the end of the fifth year of primary school (11 years of age). This research primarily deals with the first level of language proficiency (A1), which is in this case the age of young school children (as they form attitudes towards other languages and cultures at this age).

The main research aim

The main aim of this research is to identify, analyse and explain theoretically what and how cultural aspects are taught in English language lessons in primary education in Slovakia (A1 level according to the CEFR). The aim is to find out the extent, contents, methods, techniques and materials used for developing the pupils' intercultural communicative competence.

Further research aims

1. to analyse the Slovak curricular documents for teaching English at primary school level and to compare them with the CEFR considering the implementation of cultural teaching within English language education,
2. to compare the pre-reform Slovak curriculum (2001) with the current Slovak curriculum (national curriculum) concerning the implementation of cultural teaching within English language education,
3. to outline the real situation through observation and interviews of English lessons at primary school level in Slovakia, concerning the implementation of cultural teaching (extent, contents, methods, techniques and materials),

The research questions with regard to the main aim

1. How are the recommended cultural contents from CEFR reflected in the current Slovak curriculum?
2. Which techniques are used for cultural teaching in English lessons in primary education in Slovakia?
3. What materials are used for cultural teaching in English lessons in primary education in Slovakia?

Further research questions

1. To what extent do the Slovak curricular documents reflect the CEFR concerning the implementation of cultural teaching within English language education and is there a positive shift in the current curriculum in comparison to the pre-reform curriculum?
2. Where do the Slovak teachers get guidance and information from for their cultural teaching?
3. Which aspects of culture do English teachers in Slovakia prefer to teach?
4. How do the Slovak teachers reflect their own intercultural communicative competence?

2. Defining the main areas and concepts of research

In order to outline the current research coherently, it is important to first give the-oretical explanations and background for my research concerning the concept and role of culture in foreign language education; methods, techniques and materials for teaching culture; and research carried out in related areas. Professor Michael Byram is the most cited academic in this work, as he is considered to be one of the most significant specialists in the area of acquiring intercultural competences within for-eign language education. He has published numerous books and articles on inter-cultural studies, foreign language learning, education for intercultural citizenship, teaching and assessing intercultural communicative competence, cultures, etc.

1.1. Concept of culture in foreign language education

There is a great variety of possibilities and occasions for people to use a foreign language. Nowadays, people are travelling outside the boundaries of their own countries more and more and are thus coming into contact with members of dif-ferent cultures, where they have an opportunity not only to use a foreign language, but also use the skills of intercultural communication. Intercultural communica-tion is therefore a very important part of foreign language education.

Researching relationships between languages and cultures is a rich source of knowledge for foreign language education. It is not important in foreign language education to demonstrate the influence of language on the way people think and act, or vice versa, but it is important to know that language, thinking and culture are inseparable elements, which have to be learnt together.

In the past, people learned foreign languages by studying their literature, and this was the main medium of culture. It was through reading that students gained asso-ciations with the target culture (Lessard-Clouston 1997). In the Renaissance period one of the first historically documented examples of relating language and cultural content appeared. That was because of commercial trading between different coun-tries. Apprentices during their training went to foreign offices to acquire trading knowledge along with language skills (Buttjes, Byram, 1990). Another early exam-ple of interrelations between language and culture can be found in the teaching by

Comenius. He introduced the term "realia" and developed an educational philosophy that introduced the child to "the great common world" through a combination of visual and linguistic representation. Later these two approaches were forgotten. Mager's theory from the first half of the 19th century (in Buttjes, Byram, 1990) integrates language, literature and culture in the foreign language teaching with the aim to transcend the barriers of nationalistic consciousness. In the second half of the 19th century, modern languages were established as school subjects, but the cultural dimension of foreign language teaching was only a minority element.

After the first world war foreign language education was considered useful for public service and commerce, but it also served as a form of cultural education for the citizens. Besides language and literature, it included history, politics and economics in order to offer historically enlightened and more comprehensive views of the foreign culture. From the 1950s many educators started discussing the importance of including cultural aspects in foreign language teaching, putting greater emphasis on sociolinguistics and the situational context of a foreign language. The social studies model for foreign language teaching was accepted. Foreign language teaching was seen to contribute to democratic political education by offering social and international topics based on non-fiction texts and newspaper articles (Hammerly 1982; Seelve 1984; Damen 1987). The communicative approach in teaching became more apparent in the 1970s, which resulted in the more natural integration of language and culture. It recognized the sociolinguistic setting of language and language teaching as a social event (Canale, Swain 1980). In the 1980's culture started being considered and valued as a vital component of successful language learning, but linguistic proficiency kept its superiority in acquiring a foreign language (Byram 1994). Advances in pragmatics and sociolinguistics have contributed to the development of teaching culture by attempting to bridge the cultural gap in language teaching (Valdes 1986). Progress was obvious in the educators' consideration of culture as an evident element in foreign language learning, but problematic issues remained, in that they saw it as another skill rather than an integral part of communicative competence which every individual should gain, and that cultural knowledge should be an educational objective in its own right (Thanasoulas 2001).

With the introduction of the Common European Framework of Reference for Languages by the Council of Europe (CEFR, 2001) much greater importance is given to cultural components in foreign language education. A new "European" perspective was introduced into foreign language teaching with the title "Language Learning for European Citizenship". The intention is to strengthen the individual's independence of thought and action, and to make learners more socially responsible in a more pluralist society. The concept of mobility between countries is fundamental in acquiring intercultural competence.

14

The Common European Framework (2001) puts emphases on teaching cultural aspects in the foreign language classroom. It states that empirical knowledge relating to day-to-day living is essential for the management of language activities in a foreign language. These are also culturally related, as day-to-day living varies from culture to culture. However, knowledge of the shared values and beliefs (religious beliefs, taboos, assumed common history, etc.) held by social groups in other countries and regions are essential to intercultural communication. Consequently, the ability to communicate effectively with members of other cultures requires a good knowledge of the foreign language, their culture and also an awareness of the peculiarities which may occur as a result of the variation between individuals.

Hallett (1997) developed a model "the Bilingual Triangle" of acquiring intercultural competence in bilingual education. He focused on three factors: facts and phenomena about one's own country and culture (L1 culture – pupils have to know their own country and culture in order to understand foreign cultures), facts and phenomena about the target language country (L2 – pupils should be taught about different cultural aspects of the target language culture with regard to other perspectives offered on historical, current as well as future matters), culturally dependant, intercultural and global phenomena and facts (intercommunity). This means that students have to concern themselves with culturally independent, cross-cultural and universal aspects in a globalized world, comparing similarities as well as differences. This model of the Bilingual Triangle is closely connected with the method of Content and Language Integrated Learning (CLIL).

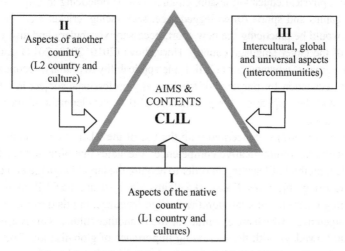

Figure 1: Hallett's Bilingual Triangle Model (1997, p. 2)

Byram (1997) also suggests ways of learning a foreign language in other curricular subjects, which has parallels with the method of CLIL. The foreign language becomes the medium of instruction of the particular subject, and not the target. Different subjects provide opportunities for the comparison of one's own and the other culture's pre-suppositions, e.g. history lessons can offer different interpretations of the same historical events (e.g. in the case of the national memory of Joan of Arc, the story has two versions, the English and French, which are both understandably quite different). Pupils acquire general knowledge, which could become relative on the bases of specific examples, which would consequently include the critical reflexion of their own society's "general historical truth". This model engages foreign language teaching/learning with the contents of other subjects, including the development of intercultural competences.

CLIL does not only bring revolutionary developments to an existing educational system, but it also creates opportunities for learners to become prepared for a successful life in multilingual and multicultural Europe. Pokrivcaková, Menzlová and Farkašová (2010) state that the concept of CLIL covers all forms of teaching artistic, technical and vocational subjects through teaching in a language, which is not the mother tongue of pupils. They also claim that apart from foreign language communicative competences, intercultural competences are also developed by the appropriate use of the CLIL method. According to Pokrivčáková (2008), CLIL also helps to develop the intercultural communicative competences of learners. Cultural aspects of the target language country and content of the subject can be combined. For example in a physical education lesson, children can be practicing in English typical English games and sports (three legged race, sack racing, cricket etc.). Here, the learners would be practicing the new sport, necessary vocabulary and also cultural aspects of the target language country. Horváthová (2010, 2013, 2014) states that one of the greatest advantages of CLIL is the applicability to primary, secondary and university education for purposes of teaching any professional subject in a foreign language and she emphasises the potential of CLIL in development of intercultural communication.

Dakowska (2007) is concerned with the use of the CLIL method in acquiring the intercultural communicative competence. She states that bilingual teaching is an efficient method of teaching in order to acquire the target language and content subject learning objectives. Dakowska claims that by using the CLIL method, i.e. by teaching other subjects through the foreign language, pupils develop intercultural competences, which are essential for life in another culture. This is especially important nowadays with the increasing importance of globalisation. This is one of the main reasons why CLIL is extremely popular throughout Europe. Pupils also learn to critically analyse the contents of lessons in L1 and L2 and gain access to other perspectives. Dakowska's research in Poland proves, that children learning in both, the mother tongue and the foreign language, are more able to understand texts, analyse them in depth and interpret them. She claims that CLIL is the most efficient form of teaching when learning a foreign language.

There is an obvious connection between using the CLIL method and cultural teaching. As it is recommended by many scholars to combine the two, there is not always a possibility to use culture in every subject or topic. However, I believe that culture should be always included when the subject and topic allow it.

When describing culture most people refer to literature, history, geography, architecture, art, or food. However there are deeper layers of culture which can be described in several ways. According to Kramsch (1993) there are two perspectives influencing the teaching of culture. One level includes factual information, and she calls it the "highbrow culture", or intellectual, elite culture. The second level includes information about customs, traditions, day-to-day life, and she calls it the "lowbrow culture", or uncultivated culture.

A similar notion of culture is presented by Stern (1993) who differentiates between the "C" (capital C) culture and the "c" (small c) culture. The "C" culture describes the elite culture, including literature, the arts, architecture and science of the particular society. The "c" culture refers to the ways of life of a particular society, their values, manners, eating habits, differences between men's and women's lives, ways of spending free time, etc., and these consequently determine the use of language discourse in communities.

Hendrich (1988) differentiates "realia" and "linguo-realia". The "realia" are characterized by the knowledge of the geography and the history as well as the economic, politic and social conditions of the particular country, including its literature, arts, science and technology. The knowledge of the "linguo-realia" should help to understand the peculiarities of the foreign language, especially those, which are connected with the way of life in the particular country.

A very eloquent analogy is Brembec's iceberg concept of culture (in Levine and Adelman, 1993; Afs Intl, 1984), where like an iceberg, the greater part is hidden below the surface. The main idea of this model is that only the top part is visible and that means fine arts, literature, music, folklore, theatre, architecture, food, clothes, holidays, etc. The greater part below the water is invisible, which is actually the foundation of the whole iceberg and it includes conversational patterns, language, dialects, accents, interaction between sexes, generations, social groups, perception of the self and others, body language, gestures, mimics, proxemics, eye contact, voice loudness, etc. The visible part is a result of the invisible part.

17

People from other cultures usually only see the visible part of the iceberg and are consciously aware of that dimension of a particular culture, but they are not able to understand the whole iceberg with its invisible parts, which are by far the most significant factors of any culture. However, with effective intercultural education, we can acquire and develop knowledge, opinions and attitudes desirable for interaction with representatives of other cultures.

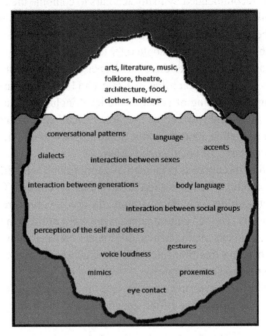

Figure 2:   Adapted visualisation of Brembec's iceberg concept of culture (in Levine and Adelman, 1993; Afs Intl, 1984)

The differentiation of culture to the "highbrow" or "lowbrow" culture, or the "C culture" or "c culture", or "realia" or "linguorealia", or "visible" or "invisible" part of the cultural iceberg, shares more or less the same criteria. All of these divisions are based on two levels of comprehension, where one level is more visible, more easily attainable than the other level. The importance is that both levels are equally significant and the intercultural communicator has to be equally competent in both levels and all their aspects. The aim of foreign language education is not only for its learners to acquire communicative competence, but also to acquire intercultural communicative competence by including cultural aspects in foreign language lessons. Without knowing the cultural specifics of the target country we cannot acquire intercultural communicative competence in the target language. Teaching language and culture should not be separated, and consequently intercultural communicative competence becomes the key competence of foreign language education.

2.2. Communicative competence in connection with culture and foreign language learning

Communicative competence is one of the targets of foreign language education. Curricular documents proposed by the European Union set several levels of competences, which pupils should obtain during their schooling. The priority of language teaching/learning is to develop pupils' competences.

The Common European Framework for Languages: Learning, Teaching, Assessment (SEFR, 2001) was created by the Council of Europe as the main part of the project "Language Learning for European Citizenship". A European Union Council Resolution (November 2001) recommended the use of this Council of Europe instrument in setting up systems of language competence. The CEFR provides a guideline for the elaboration of language syllabi, curriculum guidelines, examinations, textbooks, etc. for all European countries. It describes what the language learners have to learn in order to use the language for communication, and what knowledge and skills they have to develop to be able to act effectively in intercultural situations. CEFR (ibid.) defines six reference levels of the language proficiency, which allow learners' progress to be measured at each stage of learning. These reference levels are becoming wildly accepted as the European standard.

The CEFR (ibid.) defines general competences and communicative language competences. General competences are a sum of knowledge, skills and characteristics, which are called upon for actions of all kinds, including language activities. General competences of language learners consist of their knowledge, skills and the existential competence and their ability to learn. Knowledge (declarative knowledge) is understood as empirical knowledge from experience and academic knowledge from learning. Skills and "know-how" are related to the ability to carry out procedures (e.g. to communicate in a foreign language). We acquire skills through repetition and experience. Initially, practicing the procedures requires a high level of concentration and self-awareness (one's own self-image is vulnerable, because of the risk of failure, or of appearing incompetent). Once the skills have been acquired, a learner feels more at ease and more self-confident. The existential competence is the sum of individual characteristics, personality features and attitudes (self-image of individuals, one's view of others, willingness to engage with other people in social interaction). These have to be taken into account in language teaching/learning. The existential competence is culturally related and therefore it is very sensitive for intercultural perceptions (e.g. the way a member of one culture expresses friendliness may be considered as offense in another culture).

Communicative language competences can be understood as a system of linguistic, sociolinguistic and pragmatic components. Linguistic competences include lexical, phonological, syntactic knowledge and skills. Sociolinguistic competences refer to the socio-cultural conditions of the language use. These include rules of behaviour and politeness, norms defining relations between generations, sexes, classes and social groups. Sociolinguistic components strictly influence all language communication between members of different cultures, even though the participants are often unaware of the effect. Pragmatic competences are concerned with the functional use of linguistic resources, the mastery of discourse, phrases, idioms, offers, requests, encouragements, irony, intonation, identification of text types and forms. Pragmatic competences have a greater impact on interaction in intercultural settings than linguistic competences, as misunderstandings can occur very easily, when learners or users of a foreign language tend to use their own cultural conventions in foreign language communication (CEFR, 2001).

Additionally, the skills of non-verbal communication are a necessary component of a communicative competence. Non-verbal communication includes paralinguistics, such as body language: gestures – shaking a fist, using the middle finger; facial expressions – smile, scowl; body posture – slouching, sitting upright; eye contact – winking, staring; body contact – hand shake, kissing; proxemics – space between partners in communication; extra-linguistic speech sounds carry conventionalized meanings outside the phonological system (e.g. "pst" for requesting silence in Slovak and "sh" for requesting silence in English); prosodic qualities (such as voice quality, pitch and loudness) (CEFR, 2001). According to Byram (1997), the skills of non-verbal communication are rarely taught, or on a very superficial level. Byram (ibid.) focuses on variations in non-verbal communication between different cultures, and potential misunderstandings and confusions. He points out that the aspects of non-verbal communication are acquired in natural cultural environments, and very often unconsciously. The foreign language learner is not always able or willing to change these aspects, which he/she considers as a part of his/her personality. The aim is not to imitate aspects of non-verbal communication of the target language, but to develop the ability of the learner to recognize similarities and differences and to establish a relationship between one's own and foreign cultural systems. According to Poyatos (1992), traditional foreign language teaching concerns only a narrow area of verbal communication. Foreign language teachers should be concerned not only with language teaching, but also with paralanguage and kinetics, which are a part of the broader context of cultural signs.

Proficient User	C2	Can understand with ease virtually everything heard or read. Can summarise information from different spoken and written sources, reconstructing arguments and accounts in a coherent presentation. Can express him/herself spontaneously, very fluently and precisely, differentiating finer shades of meaning even in more complex situations.
	C1	Can understand a wide range of demanding, longer texts, and recognise implicit meaning. Can express him/herself fluently and spontaneously without much obvious searching for expressions. Can use language flexibly and effectively for social, academic and professional purposes. Can produce clear, well-structured, detailed text on complex subjects, showing controlled use of organisational patterns, connectors and cohesive devices.
Independent User	B2	Can understand the main ideas of complex text on both concrete and abstract topics, including technical discussions in his/her field of specialisation. Can interact with a degree of fluency and spontaneity that makes regular interaction with native speakers quite possible without strain for either party. Can produce clear, detailed text on a wide range of subjects and explain a viewpoint on a topical issue giving the advantages and disadvantages of various options.
	B1	Can understand the main points of clear standard input on familiar matters regularly encountered in work, school, leisure, etc. Can deal with most situations likely to arise whilst travelling in an area where the language is spoken. Can produce simple connected text on topics which are familiar or of personal interest. Can describe experiences and events, dreams, hopes and ambitions and briefly give reasons and explanations for opinions and plans.

Basic User	A2	Can understand sentences and frequently used expressions related to areas of most immediate relevance (e.g. very basic personal and family information, shopping, local geography, employment). Can communicate in simple and routine tasks requiring a simple and direct exchange of information on familiar and routine matters. Can describe in simple terms aspects of his/her background, immediate environment and matters in areas of immediate need.
	A1	Can understand and use familiar everyday expressions and very basic phrases aimed at the satisfaction of needs of a concrete type. Can introduce him/herself and others and can ask and answer questions about personal details such as where he/she lives, people he/she knows and things he/she has. Can interact in a simple way provided the other person talks slowly and clearly and is prepared to help.

Table 1:   Common Reference Levels: global scale (CEFR, 2001, p. 24)

Hymes (1972) also deals with the concepts of communicative competence in foreign language learning. He claims that if we want to master a foreign language, we have to acquire not only a grammatical competence, but also a skill to use the language appropriately. He draws attention to the importance of the sociolinguistic competence, which he considers as a base for the development of communicative language learning.

Průcha (2010, p. 126) defines communication in a foreign language as an ability to understand, express and mediate ideas, thoughts, feelings, facts and opinions in an oral or written form in social or cultural situations, while learning, working, during free time, or depending on the needs and demands of the particular individual. Communication in a foreign language equally requires abilities, which enable learners to understand their culture. This definition emphasises verbal communication and includes intercultural competence, but fails to mention non-verbal communication.

According to the Council of Europe (2001), there has to be a connection between communicative competence and intercultural competence. Communicative competence is related to the person's ability to communicate linguistically, socio-linguistically and pragmatically in a foreign language. Intercultural communicative competence is in fact an integration of communicative competence and intercultural competence.

All of the above mentioned authors share the same belief, that cultural aspects are a relevant part of communicative competence. It is not sufficient to only master the linguistic aspects of a foreign language, but it is also necessary to acquire the skills of non-verbal communication, sociolinguistic, social and pragmatic competences for successful communication in a foreign language.

2.3. Intercultural competence (IC) and Intercultural communicative competence (ICC) in education

The terms of intercultural competence and intercultural communicative competence are often used interchangeably. Even though they are both concerned with intercultural communication, Byram (1997) distinguishes between them and for this work, I consider his differentiation suitable.

Byram (1997) analyses and distinguishes both, intercultural competence and intercultural communicative competence. Byram (1997, p. 70) defines intercultural competence as "the individuals' ability to interact in their own language with people from another country and culture, drawing upon their knowledge about intercultural communication, their attitudes of interest in otherness and their skills in interpreting, relating and discovering". Namely, individuals have to overcome cultural differences and enjoy the intercultural contact. Another example of intercultural competence is the individual's ability to interpret a translated document from another culture. This does not require knowledge of the language but involves the skills of interpreting and relating, and knowledge, interests and attitudes towards the other culture.

Byram (1997, p. 71) states that someone with intercultural communicative competence "is able to interact with people from another country and culture in a foreign language. Their knowledge of another culture is linked to their language competence through their ability to use language appropriately". Such a communicator is not only able to interact successfully with others, but also to act as a mediator between people of different cultural origins. According to Byram (1997), linguistic, sociolinguistic, pragmatic and intercultural competences are components of intercultural communicative competence (ICC). He emphasises that all the learners of foreign languages need to acquire ICC, as they need it for interaction with people of different cultural identities, social backgrounds, values and manners. Unlike intercultural competence, language proficiency is the key component of intercultural communicative competence.

The aim of foreign language teaching/learning is to acquire and develop the intercultural communicative competence of its learners. ICC represents interpersonal relationships, in which communication is perceived as effective and satisfactory for all parties. Rather than promoting the notion of the native speaker as a model for foreign language learners, Byram (1997) suggests that it is better to become a competent intercultural speaker in a given situation, rather than striving to achieve the unattainable goal of the native speaker competence. Someone with ICC corresponds to the needs and opportunities of a foreign language learner with the personal experience of interaction with people from another culture involving the use of a foreign language. The knowledge of another culture is linked to language competence (the ability to use the language appropriately – awareness of the specific meanings, values and connotations of the language).

Concluding the above mentioned definitions, intercultural competence does not fulfil the needs of foreign language teaching. Intercultural competence is nevertheless a very important competence to acquire, but it is more connected with the subjects of citizenship education, history, geography and ethics, which should provide the means for the development of intercultural competences. Consequently the aim of foreign language education is to acquire intercultural communicative competence.

2.4. The role of culture within English language education

There are different views on the role of the English language in the world of international communication, business and societies, and also in foreign language education. The majority of scholars agree on the importance of including culture in the English language education (Byram, 1989, 1997; Dunnett, Dubin, Lezberg, 1986; Kramsch, 1993, 1998; Brooks, 2001; Cullen, 2000; Straub, 1999; Robinson, 1988; Huhn, 1978), but it is also believed that English has become a lingua franca and should be detached from the culture of the countries of origin (Richards, 2001).

According to Byram (1989), there is a tendency to treat language independently of the culture and this tendency disregards the nature of language. Teaching culture should not be considered as an extra fifth skill in addition to teaching speaking, listening, reading and writing. It should be always in the background, right from the beginning, to make evident the limitations of the learners' communicative competence and to challenge their ability to understand the world around them (Kramsch 1993). Consequently from the beginning we should include cultural activities to enrich the learners' awareness, attitudes, knowledge and skills concerning their own culture but also other cultures, which are needed for successful intercultural communication.

Dunnett, Dubin, Lezberg (1986) focus on the implementation of an intercultural perspective within English language lessons. This can be made by setting up courses or activities that focus on culture-related themes. Consequently, all teachers must possess a certain understanding about the culture and the language. Dunnet, Dubin, Lezberg (ibid., p. 149) discuss six aspects of understanding the importance of the relationship between languages and cultures:

- Languages cannot be translated word for word. All languages have idiomatic expressions which carry cultural connotations that are beyond the meanings of the individual words.
- The tone of a speaker's voice carries meaning (intonation pattern). All languages have different patterns of intonation. Also the degree of loudness differs from culture to culture.
- Each language – culture is concerned with gestures and body movements which also importantly convey meaning. Gestures and body movements do not always mean the same in different languages and cultures.
- Languages use different grammatical elements for describing all parts of the physical world.
- All cultures have taboo topics. Proficiency in a foreign language means knowing what one can and cannot say to whom and on what occasions.
- In personal relationships, the terms for addressing people vary considerably among different languages.

According to Dunnett, Dubin and Lezberg (ibid.) most of the English as a foreign language programmes should be revised considering the implementation of the intercultural approach to language teaching. They claim, that the major portion of the teaching time is devoted to the development of the four basic language skills and that it is often difficult to convince the English teachers that the teaching of culture is not a secondary goal. Intercultural activities should be given the same importance in the curriculum as all other language activities. If this is not done students will consider intercultural activities as secondary to language teaching and the teachers will only pay a little attention to the cultural components. The implementation of the intercultural approach in foreign language teaching requires not only a re-examination of the traditional curricula, but also the content of teacher training programmes. While a lot of attention is paid to the theoretical backgrounds of foreign language teaching, and linguistics, very little attention is paid to intercultural training. For example, students should not only have the competence to use language linguistically appropriately, but they must also be aware of the proper linguistic performance in diverse types of intercultural settings.

According to Politzer (Brooks 2001) language teachers must be interested in the study of culture not because they necessarily want to teach the culture of another country, but because they have to teach it. The reason is that if we taught language without teaching culture at the same time, we would be teaching meaningless symbols or symbols to which students would add the wrong meanings. Students would associate their own concepts with the foreign symbols. Brooks

(2001) claims that intercultural competences could be best gained in practice, just like learners acquire phonological accuracy, syntax or morphology through actual practice. Successful conversational topics should be about daily tasks which should highlight identity, similarity, or sharp differences in comparable patterns of culture (greetings, patterns of politeness, intonation patterns, taboos, festivals, music, cleanliness, etc.). Cullen (2000) warns about teaching culture with only pleasant aspects. Activities and materials should portray different aspects of culture to show contrasts within one culture (historical vs. modern, facts vs. behaviour, old vs. young people, attractive vs. shocking, etc.).

Huhn (1978) established several criteria dealing mainly with the content of cultural education:

- providing accurate, contemporary and factual information,
- relativization of stereotypes - making learners conscious of them,
- presentation of a realistic picture, not to pretend the foreign society is problem-free,
- learners should not be encouraged to accept the dominant image of the society, but to question and compare whether it is different or similar to their own culture,
- presentation of structural and functional contexts rather than isolated facts,
- presentation of historical material in relation with contemporary society. It should be made clear that the contemporary world is a result of historical development.

The importance lies though in teaching target cultural aspects in contrast and comparison with one's own cultural issues. By comparisons pupils do not only learn about the target language culture, but become more aware of their own culture, with its positives and negatives.

The norms of certain behaviour are set entirely within the particular culture and help the individuals to interpret experience in that culture. Individuals cannot use the same norms of behaviour outside their own culture expecting they would function the same. Individuals need to be aware of the existence of other cultures and of the fact that other individuals would perceive them in turn as the ones from the outside. Individuals establish social identities which they support through identifying distinctive and critical features of their cultures which serve to separate them from outsiders (Byram 1989). Culture either includes or excludes. It is hard to say who is an insider or who is an outsider, as it is hard to say what represents a particular culture. Usually members of a certain community consider themselves as insiders and others as outsiders (Kramsch 1998).

As a result of ignoring the differences between cultures, tension can occur between one's own culture and the target cultures. The tension can come from the belief that meanings which are often taken for granted are suddenly questioned and challenged (Kramsch 1993). Speakers have expectations of certain behaviour, which have originated from their experience and consequently they interpret situations based on their own culture. Perception of time can be interpreted differently by different cultures, for example when a representative of one culture expects the arrangements to be binding, while a representative of another culture does not put much importance on the exactness of being on time (German/Spanish). Rules of politeness concerning offering/accepting a refreshment can be interpreted differently, when a representative of one culture believes the refreshment should be offered several times before accepting one, while a representative of another culture offers a refreshment once and believes the visitor should accept it or refuse it. (Arab person visiting a western house, being offered a drink once, says no and gets nothing. His culture requires offering a drink several times before accepting one). Politeness or rudeness can be put to a question in the case of strangers meeting coincidentally face to face, when representatives of one culture smile or even greet one another, while representatives of another culture behave indifferently, or even look away from each other. (American, English strangers smile at each other when they meet face to face, Slovaks do not. American/English people in Slovakia might interpret the encounters as if they had offended someone, or that the Slovaks are rude.) As a result, it would be reasonable to highlight the importance of increasing the awareness of different rules of behaviour, politeness and interpretation in different cultures. This would no doubt further enrich the students' intercultural competence and enable then to develop and hone their sensitivity towards other cultures.

Kramsch (1993) claims that to learn a foreign language is not only to gain the ability to communicate but also to discover how much leeway the target language allows the learners to manipulate sounds, grammatical and syntactical forms, meanings, social norms, conversational patterns, etc. to be understood and not to be considered unfriendly or even rude. Here are some examples of common Slovak mistakes representing a combination of cultural and linguistic issues. The distinction between the vowel sounds æ/e does not exist in the Slovak language, so Slovak people tend to consider them as allophones. Mixing these sounds for example in a word *bag* /bæg - beg/ can change the meaning of the original word *bag* to *beg*. The consonant sounds d/t, or g/k are the sounds of assimilation in Slovak (voiced consonants in the final position often assimilate to the voiceless pair consonant), and if the rules of Slovak assimilation are applied into English, it can cause misunderstanding, e.g. a word *bride* /braɪd/ would be assimilated to *bright* /braɪt/, or the word *dog* /dɒɡ/ would be assimilated to *dock* /dɒk/. By using the wrong intonation patterns people can sound rude, for example if foreigners use a rising tone for example in the following sentence *Ten pounds please.* The tone naturally used by native speakers would be a falling tone, which represents a polite request. The rising tone, which is often used by foreigners, sounds very inappropriate and offensive. Grammatically it is correct to use double negative in Slovak and the meaning still would be negative. The example: *I don't have no friends* (meaning "I have no friends") is a common mistake with Slovak learners conveying just the opposite of the intended meaning. Considering tenses in the Slovak language there is no equivalent of a present perfect tense and the present tense is often used instead: *I'm learning English for three years* (meaning "I've been learning English for three years"). So using the present tense in such a sentence is highly unsuitable. It is common to omit the subject in the Slovak language, which is wrong in the English language: *Is important to pay attention.* (meaning "It's important to pay attention"), *Is really good.* (meaning "He/she/it is really good"). Omitting articles and misusing prepositions are two very common mistakes made by Slovak learners. Omitting articles or using articles inappropriately often changes the meaning of the sentence and the native speaker when listening must try to discern which alternative the speaker means. This can lead to linguistic and cultural misunderstanding (e.g. when a learner says "the man is outside", the native speaker thinks "Which man? Do I know him? Did I forget?"). Also prepositions can be culturally inappropriately used, even though grammatically they are correct. Slovaks often say "I'm going on the toilet" instead of "I'm going to the toilet", which is a literal translation from the Slovak language, but the English native speaker would perceive that as very unsuitable, perhaps even as information which is culturally and socially taboo. Different countries have different degrees of politeness. The question *Would you like tea or coffee?* could be answered *I'll have a cup of tea* in Slovak, but would be unsuitable in English. The correct answer is *I'll have a cup of tea, please.* The mentioned examples are just some of the common linguistic mistakes of the Slovak learners, which can cause not only linguistic, but also cultural misunderstandings (Reid, 2010).

According to Robinson (1988) we have to be aware of the fact that cultures never remain static, but that they are constantly changing. Cultures change over time, where different generations interpret things differently. Culture is a dynamic system of symbols and meanings where the past experiences influence meanings, which in turn affect future experiences, which subsequently influence the future meanings. Changes in culture can also be seen between generations within the same culture, where older generations do not understand the symbols of younger generations and vice versa. For example older generations do not recognize abbreviations/slang used in sms and email communication (c=see, u=you, y=why, ASAP=as soon as possible, ttyl=talk to you later, lol=laughing out loud), which are used by the young generations. This dynamic change in culture is underrated in foreign language teaching and learners work on the assumptions based on their own culture (Straub 1999). In order to attempt to understand the target language culture, we need to be aware of the changes in our own culture and to be aware that all cultures go through changes.

The opposite notion of the English language in the today's world is represented by Richards (2001). He claims that nowadays, because English is becoming the language of globalization, international communication, commerce and trade, media and pop culture, different motivations for learning English come into play. English is no longer viewed as the property of the English speaking world, but as an international commodity. The cultural values of Britain and the US are seen as irrelevant to language teaching, except the specific situations in which such information is needed. The language teacher needs no longer be an expert on British and American culture and a literature specialist as well. He claims that languages should be taught for pragmatic reasons to do with maximizing the learners' chances of success in multilingual and multicultural societies.

According to Richards (ibid.), the status of the English language in foreign language education underwent significant changes. Original perceptions of its status can be summarised as follows:

- the language of English speaking countries,
- English as culturally enriching factor,
- provides native speakers with a privileged status,
- literature being an important dimension of language learning,
- teachers being the cultural informants,
- native speaker accent being the target,
- native speaker like fluency being the target.

The current status of English as perceived by Richards (ibid.) could be seen today as:

- a practical tool for communication,
- a world commodity,
- not necessarily linked to the US or British culture,
- foreign language education influenced by national values,

- mother tongue influenced accent acceptable as well as native speaker accent,
- level of comprehensibility is more important target.

I find Richard's (ibid.) ideas and assumptions too radical, as he separates the English language from its origins and makes it an item of the world's possession. I argue that the English language cannot be treated as an artificial language without its origin, history and culture, and that all these properties have to be considered when teaching English. However, there are some ideas that we could agree with, such as the refusal of the model of the native speaker considering the accent and fluency. However this concept of refusal of the native speaker as the model of language learning was already proposed by Byram (1997).

Most scholars agree on the fact, that the teaching of culture should without a doubt be a part of foreign language teaching. Culture should be an integral part of teaching reading, listening, speaking and writing and should not be treated as an extra skill. Apart from learning the foreign language, learners should increase their knowledge of the target culture in terms of the people's way of life, values, attitudes, beliefs and how these are manifested in the linguistic categories and forms. At the same time as learning about the target language culture, learners should be encouraged to critically look at their own culture, with the aim to understand that there is no such a thing as a superior or inferior culture. In order to acquire intercultural communicative competence, language teachers need to be well prepared to be able to provide learners with relevant cultural information, prepare extra activities, encourage and support learners' critical thinking and discussions. To be able to fulfil these criteria, language teachers should receive both experience and academic training, with the aim of becoming "cultural mediators".

2.5. Techniques, methods and materials used in teaching culture

In the following subchapter various views, techniques, methods and materials are discussed, which could be used in foreign language lessons to acquire and develop cultural knowledge, awareness and intercultural communicative competences.

According to Byram (1997) acquiring intercultural competence is a complex matter involving more than traditional language lessons. Also teachers might find it difficult to identify themselves with the objectives of intercultural competence. Linguists probably find it more difficult than the people educated in literary criticism, who can find analogies in the skills of interpreting and discovering with the traditions of some approaches to literature. Byram (ibid.) names three overlapping categories of location for acquiring intercultural competence: the classroom, fieldwork, and independence experience.

There is a general assumption, that classroom learning is a preparation for experience in the real world. Byram (ibid.) suggests that engagement with otherness in the contemporary world is simultaneous and that the dichotomy of the classroom and the real world is a false one. The classroom has advantages of providing systematic and structured presentation of knowledge, acquisition of knowledge and skills under the guidance of a teacher and the classroom can be the location for the reflection of skills and knowledge. One of the objectives of classroom learning is to acquire knowledge of the relationships between the different perceptions of one's own culture and the other culture. Learners should be introduced to features of the national memory of another country and how they are perceived by other societies including their own. Also skills of non-verbal communication of the target culture should be introduced. The classroom provides opportunities for teaching skills of interpreting, as knowledge and skills are inter-related. What the classroom cannot offer is the chance to develop the skills of interaction in real circumstances. The only possibility is to simulate real communication.

Pedagogically structured experience outside the classroom, in fieldwork is another way of acquiring intercultural communicative competence. Fieldwork could be a short visit organized by a teacher or learners, or a long term period of residence organized for or by the learner, who has limited contact with the teacher during the stay. Fieldwork allows the development of all the skills in real circumstances, especially the skills of interaction. In interaction, learners have a chance to experience communication under time pressures and to appreciate the significance of non-verbal behaviour. In long term fieldwork learners can especially develop attitudes including the ability to cope and engage with unfamiliar conventions, etc. This experience does not necessarily lead to learning and it is important that the teacher sets the attitude objectives (Byram, 1997). Fieldwork could be adapted to foreign language teaching, when the teaching is organized outside the classroom. This would probably involve creating situations, in which students would be using the foreign language. It would be a kind of imitation of authentic situations, but could be very effective for intercultural teaching.

Independent learning is a part of life-long learning. It can be subsequent or simultaneous with classroom learning and fieldwork. Effectiveness depends on the learners' ability to continue to develop their knowledge, skills and attitudes acquired in previous learning. Otherwise, the experience of otherness remains mere experience (Byram 1997).

For teaching cultural awareness Hughes (1986) selects some of the most practical techniques. The "comparison method" concentrates on discussing the differences between the native and target cultures. With the technique of "cultural assimilation" the learners are presented with a critical incident, which would probably be misunderstood. Learners are given four possible explanations, from which they choose the one which they think is correct. By "cultural capsule" the teacher presents learners, for example with a custom that would be different in the two cultures. It would be accompanied by visual aids to show the differences and a set of questions for class discussions. "Drama" is a technique where learners act out short scenes of misinterpretation and also clarification of something that happens between two cultures, which is caused by misunderstanding the target culture. "TPR" technique is designed to respond to oral commands to act out a cultural experience. By creating a "cultural island" (putting contemporary posters, pictures) in a classroom the teacher tries to attract the students' attention, evoke comments and maintain the cultural atmosphere. "Print media" provide a rich source of cultural aspects. Students are asked to compare items between foreign and their magazines, newspapers (headlines, advertisements, sports pages, comics, weather reports). Electronic media (radio, television, films) are a welcome variety of classroom activities and offer first-hand cultural presentations.

According to Cullen (2000) many books which attempt to teach culture offer only discussion activities. Without doubt discussion is a valuable technique for learning culture but not all the students are able to discuss complex issues in a foreign language. Cullen offers a number of various activities which would contribute to effective development of intercultural competences. "Reformulation" is retelling a story to a partner in his/ her own words. It could be a story from listening, reading or watching a video. It is a simple but successful method for both language and culture learning. "Noticing" is paying attention to particular features. For example, by identifying differences in Christmas customs depicted in a video. By asking students to notice the differences, it makes them more involved rather than passively viewing the video. "Treasure hunt" involves searching for certain items set in advance, for example people, dates, events in a news or magazine article. "Prediction" engages students actively by finishing (predicting) for example a half told story. Or the students are given only some information about the new topic and they predict what they would learn. This should evoke the students' curiosity and interest to talk, no matter if their predictions are correct or not. "Role plays" for example based on menus give learners great opportunities to practice structures and functions of the language being acquired. "Research" is one of the most powerful learning tools, which combines learning and interests. Students are asked, for example to research any aspects of the target culture that interest them, present their projects and also create and present posters. Also most of the standard EFL activities (games, role plays, field trips, singing, etc.) could be adapted for teaching culture.

Dunnett, Dubin, Lezberg (1986) suggest some teaching techniques for the development of intercultural competences. These techniques are drawn from practices with foreign students in the USA, and most of them can be well adapted for foreign language teaching in our environment. The "problem solving" technique presents students with a problem to solve. This technique evokes discussions about cultural differences. The problem could be set out elaborately with a number of points to discuss, or it can offer students alternate endings to the story and students discuss which solution is the best. An already previously mentioned technique is called "cultural assimilator". Here, an incident containing a misunderstanding between a non-native speaker of English and a native speaker is described. Students are given various interpretations coming from culturally different points of view, from which they choose what they think is the accurate one. Then they check their answers and if their interpretations are wrong, the students are given explanations of the correct interpretations. Other techniques include: the "role play" - where students take on the parts of typical members of the different cultures, "value hierarchies" - students put random lists of items into a preferred order, "comparisons and contrasts" - students fill in blanks with their choice (e.g. Who is responsible for the following household tasks in your country? mother/father/both parents/ servant/children/nobody). Another effective technique for the development of the intercultural perspective is the use of "personal diaries/journals". Students often experience their own understanding of the intercultural elements in a class discussion, when they reflect on the reactions of other students. In using any of the above mentioned techniques, it is very important to give space for full and open discussions following the activities.

Content, levels of difficulty, as well as types of material for cultural teaching should be carefully chosen. Teachers cannot just simply go to the class and teach all the cultural aspects of the target country. They have to know what their students' interests are, should ask them what they want to learn about the target culture. Teachers should therefore pick out interesting aspects from the target culture and present them in a way that would engage the learners' attention. Of course teachers' enthusiasm is important for creating exciting classes (Cullen 2000). Teachers should encourage their learners to compare the given information with their own culture, as learners tend to think that what they do in their own culture is the same in other cultures (Galloway 1981). The age, language level and background knowledge of the learners should be considered when choosing the difficulty level of cultural materials. The materials have to be comprehensible to the learners, but at the same time should be challenging enough to sustain their motivation. Therefore, selected materials should be at an equal level of difficulty or slightly above the learners' present level. Teachers have to remember that the learners would not presumably understand everything presented. Consequently, it is not the aim to understand every word, but to challenge the learners to want to learn more about the target country, to encourage learners to pursue their studies of the language and the culture of the respective country and above all to raise intercultural awareness (Cullen 2000).

Creating a portfolio could be a valuable means of keeping control over one's own progression. It documents improvements in competence, maintains the relationship between testing and teaching, as the documentation is done in the teaching and learning process. A portfolio allows levels to be set for each component and for holistic performance. It can contain examination results, the specification of examined skills, an example of a translation from the foreign language with the teacher's evaluation, the understanding of various aspects of the foreign culture, a description of encounters with someone in the foreign language, the learner's experience from visiting a foreign country, a description of the learner's experience both within and outside formal learning, etc. Additionally, the portfolio can be used as a passport to further educational opportunities (Byram 1997).

Byram (1997) suggests that the selection of documents, authentic or contrived, involving generalizing and stereotyping statements could be included in an accessible language in the foreign language lesson. The documents should be suitable for the easy analysis of ethnocentric perspectives in order to start the development of skills of interpreting and relating, identification of values and developing critical views. By analysing documents, which include ethnocentric views of familiar stereotypes, learners should critically compare their own perspectives of another culture to similar stereotypes of their own culture. This should help to initiate the development of understanding in individual learners.

There is a vast amount of materials that could be used in teaching culture. Authentic materials are one of the most attractive sources for foreign language classrooms. Harmer (1991) describes authentic texts (written or spoken) as those which are designed for native speakers, they are real texts designed not for language students, but for the speakers of the language in question. Most everyday objects in the target language qualify as authentic materials. According to Nunan and Miller (1995) authentic materials are those which were not created or edited for language learners. Authentic materials bring reality to the classroom and all the learners can

34

make contact with the real-life language, which can be a great motivational factor for them. Authentic materials introduce learners to the reality of the language, help them to recognize that there is a community of users who live their lives in this other language. Exposing learners to authentic materials can also help them understand the target culture and imagine how they might participate in this community. On the level of day to day teaching of foreign languages, authentic materials can make individual lessons more interesting or remarkable especially for teaching phrasal verbs, idioms and particular culturally specific phrases (Brinton D., Wong A. 2009).

Authentic materials include "audio materials" (TV programmes, commercials, news, weather reports, films, cartoons, radio programmes including adverts, music, audio materials on the internet, audio-taped stories and novels, announcements at the airports, shops, etc.), "visual materials" (photographs, paintings and drawings, wordless street signs, images on the internet, pictures from magazines, postcards, stamps, coins, wordless picture books, etc.), "printed materials" (newspapers including adverts, magazines, TV guides, books, catalogues, lyrics to songs, restaurant menus, product labels, street signs, tourist information brochures, maps, letters, junk mail, school notices, billboards, bus and train schedules, application forms, printed materials on the internet, etc.).

Although there is a great choice of available authentic materials, teachers need to be careful in choosing appropriate materials for foreign language teaching, which include suitable cultural contents. Teachers should set up specific criteria for selecting materials suited to the special group of learners. They have to make sure that the topic of the authentic materials meets the needs and interests of the specific group of learners. There is a need to take into account the age, language level, interests, usefulness and background of the learners. Cultural appropriateness has to be considered, as authentic materials are based on native speakers' culture which may be quite alien or inappropriate to some language learners. Teachers have to consider whether the students have the background knowledge for the topic and if the information included in the materials has any value to the students (Reid, 2009).

Authentic materials, especially from the internet are easily and inexpensively obtainable. The internet is a rich source of all kinds of authentic materials, including audio, visual and printed materials. Nuttall (1996) gives three criteria for choosing authentic texts to be used in the classroom: suitability of content, exploitability and comprehensibility. I presume, that these criteria can be used generally for choosing any authentic materials for the foreign language classroom.

- "suitability" of content can be considered as the most important. Authentic materials should be interesting and relevant to the needs of the learners.

- "exploitability" refers to how the authentic materials can be used to develop the students' knowledge and competence. Just being authentic does not mean that it can be useful.
- "comprehensibility" refers to grammatical and lexical difficulty, it has to be appropriate to the language level of the learners.

There are many references to the use of authentic materials in ELT literature. There are many discussions whether authentic materials should or should not be included in foreign language lessons. Authors supporting the use of authentic materials have one idea in common that the learners benefit from being exposed to the language in an authentic context. There are many advantages to using authentic materials in foreign language teaching. Here the most significant ones are mentioned:

- they bring reality into the classroom, which makes interaction meaningful,
- they connect the classroom to the outside world,
- they provide authentic cultural information,
- they expose learners to a wide range of natural language,
- they are suitable for all language levels, from basic levels to advanced levels,
- they are actual with up to date topics
- research studies on the use of authentic materials have proved that there is an overall increase in motivation towards learning (Nuttall 1996).

Certainly there are also problems and disadvantages with using authentic materials. The disadvantages mentioned by several writers include:

- they can contain difficult language, unusual vocabulary which is not used in everyday life, complex language structures (Richard, 2001),
- they may be too culturally biased, too many structures mixed, causing lower levels to have problems decoding the texts,
- special preparation is necessary which can be time consuming. It requires a lot of effort to choose the right type of material and to prepare the supporting exercises,
- with listening, too many different accents and dialects,
- material can be outdated easily, e.g. news, gossip (Martinez 2002).

Despite certain disadvantages, there are still more advantages to using authentic materials in the foreign language classroom, but the potential problems should be carefully considered when choosing authentic materials. Authentic materials provide a rich source of cultural material. The chosen cultural materials should be freely discussed by learners and compared to their own culture in the relaxing atmosphere of the language classroom. If learners are regularly exposed to authentic materials, they could become more familiar with them and in the future be able to partially avoid a cultural shock when visiting the culture in question.

2.6. Intercultural education in reflection of the curricular reform in Slovakia

School systems in the USA, the UK, Holland and other countries are known for their liberalism concerning school curriculums and they give a great scope of freedom to schools in creating their school curriculums. In Slovakia, there is also an interest to create a "participating curricular politics" (state – region – school – class), where the state issues an essential declaration, that all the people are entitled to a high quality and adequate education. The state issues the "national curriculum" (Štátny vzdelávací program), which Průcha (1997, p. 250) defines as a curriculum guaranteed by the state, which is in fact a national framework intended for the whole population in the school age. It was first introduced in 1988 in the UK, and it comprises of general objectives of school education, specifies basic components of the educational contents, and gives guidelines for implementing the national curriculum at schools. As we have mentioned earlier, at present, the Slovak education system is going through curricular reform and the new School act (245/2008) was passed on 22nd May 2008. It defines the new school system and makes it compatible with other European systems. It introduces the national curriculum, which becomes the binding fundamental document for developing school curricula. Consequently, the Slovak school system has two levels of curriculum: the "national curriculum" and the "school curriculum" (Školský vzdelávací program). The national curriculum sets out the key stages, core subjects, expected standards of pupils' performance and model curricula. For each subject, there is a programme of study, which describes the subject knowledge, skills and understanding pupils are expected to develop during each key stage. The school curriculum specifies individual subjects for each stage at individual schools, respecting the distinctive characteristics of the communities and regions (Štátny vzdelávací program…, 2008).

In the school reform, foreign language education becomes one of the most significant areas of curricular modernization. The curricular reform in foreign language education should eliminate the diversity of variations of teaching plans and

37

should increase the quality of the foreign language teaching. The reform is based on the requirements of the European committee and the priority is to provide effective foreign language education for children from a very early age (8 years old), as the key attitudes towards other languages and cultures are formed at that age. The Slovak parliament passed a new concept of teaching foreign languages at primary and secondary schools (12th September 2007), which sets the compulsory teaching of two foreign languages, the first language to the third class of primary schools, and the second language to the fifth class of primary schools. The new concept also increases the amount of foreign language lessons and defines new criteria for on-going and final evaluations. The new Slovak curricular documents are based on the Common European Framework of Reference for Languages: Learning, Teaching, Assessment (2001).

The national curriculum for foreign languages emphasises the importance of discovering and understanding other cultures, which exceeds the knowledge of foreign languages. Learning foreign languages and cultures enables pupils to communicate accurately with other inhabitants of the European Union. Knowledge of foreign languages enables learners to explore differences in the life styles of people in different countries and their traditions. Tolerance and intercultural understanding should be developed in foreign language lessons. The current project contemplates the A1 level of English language proficiency and the national curriculum for this level describes the importance of the development of understanding one's own and target language cultures. More specifically, pupils should learn about traditions, ways of behaviour, polite phrases, etc. The aim of intercultural education is to create a tolerant and respectful approach to other cultures (Štátny vzdelávací program…, 2011).

2.7. Current research on intercultural communication within foreign language teaching

The following part of this chapter introduces some of the research carried out on the acquisition, development, and assessment of intercultural communicative competences (ICC), intercultural sensitivity and intercultural maturity in foreign language education.

In Slovakia, Ciprianová (2008) dealt with the integration of cultural teaching in English language education. In her research she studied how the integration of cultural content influences secondary students' attitudes and opinions. The author's analyses of curricular documents for secondary schools show that there is no systematic approach to the cultural content within language education, and the critical view of one's self and the relativization of one's own culture are missing. They do not include instructions allowing students to see beyond their own cultural reality, to become aware of other cultures, to form the ability to understand others and their cultures. There is insufficient instruction for the teachers concerning the informative and formative aims of foreign language education. The attitudes and opinion of the secondary school students were gathered from questionnaires. 143 students participated in completing the questionnaire. It is apparent from the findings, that students did not show ethnocentric attitudes and the girls showed a more positive attitude towards other cultures than the boys. The findings from the questionnaire also reject the assumption that contact with representatives of foreign cultures leads to positive attitudes. The outcome of this research also shows that the students' attitudes towards and opinions of other cultures are formed mainly by influences outside of school, especially mediated by experiences of other people. The assessed cultural content in foreign language education plays an insignificant role in the formation of positive attitudes and opinions of other cultures. Ciprianová (ibid.) considers it inevitable to define foreign language learning as a means of preparation for intercultural communication, to specify the contents of cultural teaching and students' competences at different levels and to specify the levels of intercultural communication for each grade in the curricular documents.

The following Europublic study researched a similar area of ICC in English language education. In 2006 Europublic (2007), in collaboration with an academic team from 12 European Member State universities, completed a study for the European Commission, on the intercultural skills taught in foreign language courses at each stage of compulsory education in primary and lower secondary education, called LACE, Languages and Cultures in Europe. The primary objective of this study was to identify and assess the nature, scope and extent of ICC developed in foreign language education in selected countries (Belgium, Denmark, Finland, France, Germany, Greece, Hungary, Italy, Poland, Slovenia, the UK and Norway). The objectives of the national curricula regarding the development of ICC were reviewed. The main didactic and methodological approaches recommended in the national curricula were also reviewed. This was carried out by an online survey with 213 foreign language teachers in primary and lower secondary education. Also telephone interviews were conducted with 78 teachers about their experiences of developing ICC as language teachers. The objectives of the national curricula were compared with actual classroom practices, based on the teachers' feedback. The findings reported that the national curricula paid most attention to the development of linguistic competences and communication skills, and the ICC (if included) got paid considerably less attention. However differences were found between countries and between levels. Information on didactic and methodological approaches was limited in most curricula. From the teachers' reports it was apparent that more than 80% of teachers used the oral teacher input. Between 50 to 75% of teachers said that they used role plays, task-based activities, online information, etc. Between 25 to 49% of teachers said that they used the CLIL method, simulations, games, cross-cultural dialogues, etc. Only a few teachers reported that they employed techniques of ICC development outside the language classroom. More than half of the teachers reported spending 80% of the classroom time on language learning, and 20% on developing ICC. About a third of the teachers reported that they spend 60% of the classroom time on language learning, and 40% on developing ICC. The most frequently mentioned difficulty for the teachers was the lack of time for including intercultural teaching in their lessons. 92.5% of teachers complained that there should be more specific guidance for teachers with regard to the development of ICC. Many teachers said that they would need more training for a better understanding of ICC, and that their previous teacher training was inadequate. 63.4% of teachers claimed that they had little or no training in this area in their teacher education. The outcomes from this study were recommendations at European and national levels, which included: making ICC development alongside foreign language learning a key feature for multilingualism, supporting research into the nature, development and assessment of ICC in school settings, supporting teacher mobility, school partnerships, exchanges, visits, improving teacher education concerning ICC, improving foreign language curricula in a way to include clearer and more detailed specifications of objectives, descriptions of didactic and methodological approaches and methods.

An extensive study carried out by Zerzová (2012) dealt with the development of intercultural communicative competences within English language lessons at a lower secondary school education level in the Czech Republic Video recordings were made of 79 lessons conducted by 25 different teachers. The aims of the study were to find out the frequency and quality of cultural teaching, the relationship between teaching culture and the working language, lesson arrangement, and the use of teaching aids and media for cultural teaching. The author also described curricular documents, the CEFR being the base document for elaboration of the Czech curricula. Zerzová (ibid.) remarked that policy makers talk about the development of ICC (attitudes, values and empathy), but do not say how to develop them. The observation of the contents of cultural teaching was focused on the proportion of activities which developed cognitive, behavioural and affective levels of ICC, big-C culture and small-c culture, general and specific aspects. From the analyses of video recordings, she found out that 62% of lessons did not include any cultural teaching. When it came to the cognitive level of ICC (knowledge), her findings were that all (100%) of the lessons focused on acquiring knowledge. From the teaching methods Czech teachers used for cultural teaching, the most popular were discussion (43%) and lecture (23%). Also techniques such as pair work, group work, role plays, games were present, but on a much smaller scale. The outcomes from this study illustrated a great neglect of cultural teaching in secondary schools in the Czech Republic, which might partially be a result of superficial curricular documents.

Research carried out by Kostková (2012) offers an insight into the development of ICC of university students of English language in Czech Republic. The research includes curricular document analyses and a case study of English language teacher trainees. The place of intercultural learning is analysed in the context of the Czech national curriculum and school curricula. Kostková (ibid.) claims that curricular documents do not sufficiently include development of ICC. Even though the national curriculum for the English language covers all dimensions of ICC, the dimensions are covered only superficially, without any deeper elaboration of individual dimensions. Overall, the development of ICC is included only on general basis and the curricular documents do not offer sufficient support for the language teachers. The author (ibid.) developed and executed a new study subject "Intercultural communicative competence" for university teacher trainees. The efficiency of this subject was supported by the YOGA form questionnaire and focus group discussions with the students. The research findings showed a positive development of the ICC of the teacher trainees. Kostková (ibid.) proved that the development of ICC is also possible in an artificial classroom environment. However, she pointed out that to be interculturally communicatively competent does not guarantee to be a good teacher of ICC. Consequently, there is definitely a need to create a subject, which would be didactically preparing teachers on how to develop ICC of their learners within English language lessons.

Baker (2003) in his research dealt with the position of English language in foreign language education. Even though Baker's (ibid.) research is not the most current one, it deals with one of the most current topics: should English be taught as the "lingua franca" (Richards, 2001) or a language with culture (Byram, 1989, 1997; Dunnett, Dubin, Lezberg, 1986; Kramsch, 1993, 1998; Brooks, 2001; Cullen, 2000; Straub, 1999; Robinson, 1988; Huhn, 1978). Baker (ibid.) in his study examined English language education and the teaching of culture in Thailand. In Thailand, the English language is the second language for most Thais and is often taught in schools from the first years of schooling. In many countries, such as

Thailand, English is often used as an international language rather than as a means of communicating with English speakers from English speaking countries. This brings into question the relevance of teaching English culture. However, from Baker's own experience and survey research with the university students, it was apparent that students often expressed a desire to learn about English culture. 68% of respondents cited interest in English culture as an important reason for studying English. An even greater majority of 89% remarked that they wanted to communicate with English native speakers as an important reason for studying English. Baker (ibid.) concluded that the teaching of culture should take place within the normal language classroom and not as a separate subject as had been traditionally taught in Thailand. Learners should acquire the English language together with its culture within the English lessons, and at this point culture should be discussed. Instead of just learning about the facts of one culture, the emphasis should move towards interpreting culture based on intercultural understanding, involving comparisons and contrasts with the learners' native culture and other cultures. This means, that not only the English speaking cultures should be taught, but also other cultures should be included. Teaching materials should encourage learners to compare cultures and to take a critical perspective. These can include materials drawn from English speaking cultures (newspapers, magazines, etc.), intercultural materials involving outsiders' observations on English culture (Thai newspapers, magazines, etc.), and locally produced English materials (Thai newspapers, magazines written in English). These types of materials could be used in class discussions, comparisons, research, role-plays, etc. The materials could be arranged around such objects as cultural symbols and products (e.g. popular images, architecture, landscapes, cultural behaviour, what is considered appropriate, values, attitudes, patterns of communication, non-verbal communication, feelings and experiences of the target culture, etc.). From this study it is apparent, that even though, the Thai learners might not need to know about the English speaking cultures for their use of English in the Thai environment, but that they have a desire to learn about the English speaking cultures. It is the learners' own wish to learn the language with culture and it motivates them to learn more. Once again, this study proves that foreign language learning should not be separated from cultural learning. It is necessary though to not only teach English speaking cultures, but also other cultures with the aim to develop intercultural understanding and competences.

Durocher (2007) researched the development of intercultural sensitivity on American language students learning French. Three classes were pre-tested with the Intercultural Development Inventory to evaluate their level of sensitivity to cultural differences. The reason for this research was to determine if Bennett's

(1993) recommendation to address denial and defence issues in elementary-level language classes was warranted, to incorporate intercultural training activities to the students' level of sensitivity as revealed by the inventory, and to post-test students at the end of semester to see if a noticeable increase in the level of sensitivity had been observed. The pre-tests were carried out on all the students: those who would have intercultural training and those who would not. Even though it seemed that the students were starting with different levels of sensitivity, the reality was that in both groups the majority of students were identified in one of the ethnocentric levels of sensitivity. In the control group, 71% of the students were in denial or the defence stage of sensitivity, compared to 65% of the students in the group that was to receive the intercultural training. A total of five intercultural training activities were planned and implemented during one semester. These activities were spread out at even intervals during the semester, with each activity taking about 30 minutes. All activities were addressed to the denial and defence issues. The outcome of the post-test with the class that received the training are as expected. Even though there was not a considerable shift from ethnocentric to ethnorelative levels of sensitivity, the results were still encouraging. Most students moved a level higher in the framework of intercultural sensitivity. The biggest growth was in the minimalization stage from 31 to 54%. Still, 47% of the students remained in the denial or the defence stage of sensitivity. Overall, most students were still ethnocentric, but a shift toward the ethnorelative stages of sensitivity was observed. The class that received no intercultural training experienced some changes too. The most noticeable was the shift of three students from minimalization to defence stage. This points to the fact that language classes themselves do not automatically train students toward ethnorelativism, but they can in reverse provoke defence issues and make students more ethnocentric. Durocher (ibid.) notes that if foreign language educators do not effectively address the negative attitudes of their students, they run the risk of doing more harm than good. This claim can only be agreed upon when taking into account that ethnorelativism does not naturally go hand in hand with foreign language education, and if intercultural issues are not included in foreign language lessons, then in extreme cases a reverse process can occur in which students become even more ethnocentric than before. This finding is quite alarming, and educators, especially foreign language teachers, should be aware of the danger, that omitting intercultural training can cause.

Marx (2008) carried out a case study with a teacher trainee and her intercultural sensitivity development during a one semester education study abroad program in England. The aim of the study was to seek an understanding of the ways international experiences influence teachers' intercultural development and find out if international experiences prepare culturally responsive teachers. The respondent was an American teacher trainee, who took an internship at a secondary school in a lower-income neighbourhood in London with a multicultural population of 1,400 students (ages 11–19). The respondent spent twenty hours a week as a mathematics support teacher. Qualitative data sources and collection methods namely field work, in-depth interviews and document analyses, helped the researcher to uncover the respondent's subjective experiences within the context of an intercultural environment. The findings show that at the beginning, the respondent had a slightly ethnocentric approach and showed characteristics from the minimalization stage of the developmental model of intercultural sensitivity (DMIS). This can be interpreted that she was interested in learning about other cultures, but her understanding was unsophisticated and she was seeking individual and psychological explanations for differences. Towards the end of the respondents stay abroad she adopted a more ethnorelative approach, and she moved to the acceptance stage of DMIS. This means that she developed more sophisticated cultural-constructs, explored her own cultural identity, accepted and recognized fundamental cultural differences in herself and others, and was actively seeking intercultural experiences. The respondent has, under the influence of intercultural environments, moved from the ethnocentric to the ethnorelative stage of intercultural sensitivity. The researcher thinks that this is because the respondent was an outsider within the cultural context, where her cultural values no longer applied, and she was forced to become more conscious of the host culture and cultural differences. Even though this study was not set in a foreign language education environment and the language was the same in both the country of origin and the host country, there were still intercultural differences which had to be recognized and dealt with. It is understandable that intercultural competences are best acquired in the target language country and it would be ideal if every foreign language teacher spent a considerable length of time in that country. However, it is not always possible mainly for financial reasons.

Stickler and Emke (2011) conducted a project called Literalia, which was funded by the European Union and it observed the development of intercultural maturity in adult foreign language learners. The aim of the project was to connect adult language learners (229) from four different countries (the UK, Germany, Italy and Poland) and analyse the participants' intercultural learning and show the development of intercultural maturity. The participants were working in pairs and were to give mutual support to each other in learning one another's language and culture through online communication. Qualitative data was collected by observation, feedback and interviews and analysed to present a description of the adults' experiences through intercultural learning. The findings show that the personal learning partner became the central figure and the development of friendship was the central point. The tandem partner was a trusted source of information and intercultural exploration. Learners would sometimes venture into uncomfortable zones of intrapersonal development, examining and accepting their own and other cultures in context. The research claims that intercultural maturity depends on social interaction and it is not a change in personality or life style, but an integration of new perspectives into the everyday life of the mature intercultural learner. The study focused on how interactions shaped and developed intercultural competences. The idea of connecting language learners online is a similar idea to 'penpal' friendships, only this is carried out online, which is quicker and can become very intensive. It is always a very good idea for practicing a foreign language, but it also helps cultural learning. The study shows that when the interpersonal relationship is strong, then cultural learning comes naturally.

A qualitative study carried out by Crossman (2011) reports how undergraduate and culturally diverse students experienced a collaborative, international, experiential project to learn about intercultural communication. The purpose of this research paper was to reveal how student participants in Australia experienced the project about intercultural communication through intercultural communication from their own perspective. The project involved the collaboration of first year Australian business students from mixed cultural heritages as well as international students. The total number of participants was 27 from countries such as Australia, the Netherlands, Botswana, China, Korea, India, Malaysia and Singapore. The data were collected from interviews, questionnaires and journals and they were analysed using the constant comparative method. Asian and Western students became for each other a source for learning about intercultural issues and together with theoretical literature they tried to make sense of intercultural communication. This programme also provided students with the experience of assisting one another to untangle the complex influence of culture in interpersonal communication by drawing upon and sharing the perspectives of their own cultural heritage and experience. The author concludes that this experiential learning proved to be a powerful tool for learning about intercultural communication through intercultural communication in the context of international and culturally diverse teams working on business case studies. This research was not concerned with the development of intercultural communicative competences in foreign language teaching, but it could be equally well adapted with successful results in foreign language education.

Another qualitative study by Andrew (2011) deals with the development of intercultural communicative competences of international students abroad, in

New Zealand. 70 students from China, Taiwan, Hong Kong, Sweden, Korea, Germany, Japan, Romania, Iran, Ethiopia, Somalia, Thailand, Malaysia, India, French Polynesia and Samoa took part in this research. Their average length of time in New Zealand was three years. The students were to do ten or more hours of community work, from which they were asked to write a diary commenting on their observations of any interesting aspects of New Zealand "Kiwi" culture. Participants were told to write freely and openly, rather than to create an error-free essay. The researchers used open coding to locate themes that emerged from the data. The themes were listed in order of frequency from those mentioned by the majority of participants down to those described by only several. The data reported here was collected from six semesters of research. The outcome of this research was that it provided students with the opportunities to participate in situated, real world discourse and it also provided them with authentic opportunities to develop intercultural communicative competences through socialization and practices in the community work. This is just another research project proving that spending some time in diverse culture communities develops the learners' ICC, whether they are language learners or not. Undoubtedly, the idea of students' mobility is very beneficial for development of ICC, but it is very difficult for most foreign language learners, because of the opportunities and also financial reasons.

Even though there has been a great development of theoretical models of intercultural communication and research carried out on the methods and techniques of developing intercultural communicative competences, the question remains on how much time and space is given to the cultural teaching within foreign language education. According to Allen (1985), foreign language teaching concentrates mainly on the acquisition of grammar and vocabulary. This is understandable though, as textbooks' structures are based on the grammatical concepts, and grammar and vocabulary are easily tested, as grammatical structures and vocabulary are in fact limited and rarely change. It is also easier for a language teacher to become proficient in grammar and vocabulary, than in intercultural communication, as culture is diffusive, changeable, uncatchable, and difficult to test. This is especially difficult for a teacher who is not a native speaker or does not have direct contact with the target language culture. Non-native teachers often find employing cultural content in foreign language teaching a very hard task to do and as a result they often (detrimentally) omit the cultural content. One of the goals of the current research project is to assess whether this is indeed the situation in Slovak primary schools.

The implementation of culture in foreign language education is becoming a very popular topic of research at universities in Slovakia. For example the Department of Language Pedagogy and Intercultural studies at Constantine the Philosopher

University in Nitra organizes an annual international conference "Foreign languages and cultures at schools", where a whole section "The Development of intercultural competences within foreign language education" concentrates on teaching culture within foreign language lessons at primary and secondary schools. Universities are keen to open new courses on intercultural communication for language teacher trainees, the cultural mediator and translator trainees, and new study programmes preparing cultural mediators and translators/interpreters for intercultural communication.

From the research we have come across there has only been limited research done on cultural teaching within foreign language education at a primary school level. Most of the research we have come across has been carried out with adults and has focused on their acquisition, abilities and experiences with intercultural communication. However, the research carried out by Ciprianová (2008), Zerzová (2012), Europublic (2006) and Kostková, 2012, dealt with very similar issues to the current research. Ciprianová's research was carried out at a secondary school level and the data were gathered from the analyses of curricular documents and questionnaires. The current research was carried out at a primary school level and the data was enriched by the observation of English language classes. Zerzová's research was also carried out at secondary schools, but was dealing with issues similar to the current research concerning the contents of cultural teaching. The research methods were video analyses of lessons and document analyses. Zerzova's document analyses did not go into any great depth. However, the current research sought to not only closely analyse the curricula but also importantly to compare them with the CEFR. Furthermore this analysis was complimented with classroom observations and interviews with the teachers of ELT in primary schools in Slovakia. The Europublic research was concerned with teaching culture in foreign language courses at compulsory education across some European countries. Slovakia was not a part of this study and it would be valuable to find out and compare the outcomes of the two studies. The current study wanted to go further than the Europublic research and so it included the observation of English lessons at primary schools. Kostková's (2012) research similarly to the current research analysed the national curriculum and school curricula. Kostková's (ibid.) main concern was a case study of English language teacher trainees and development of their ICC in the new study subject "Intercultural communicative competences". The current research concentrates on the primary school level, but the analyses of the national curricula can be compared.

3. An outline of the research undertaken

3.1. Methodology of the research

The educational world is full of complexity, richness and contradictions and not everything can be easily measured and counted, some things have to be understood deeply and the methods of qualitative research fulfil these criteria. The qualitative approach is usually holistic and it seeks a description and interpretation of the "total phenomena". It should be concerned more with description rather than prediction, induction rather than deduction, generation rather than verification of theory, construction rather than enumeration, and subjectivities rather than objective knowledge. The researchers become human instruments in the research, building on their tacit knowledge, using methods such as observation, interview, documentary analysis and other non-interfering methods. The advantage of human instruments are their adaptability, ability to handle sensitive things, ability to see the whole picture, ability to clarify and summarize, to explore and analyse (Cohen, Manion, Morrison, 2007). A qualitative research design was chosen for this study as the aim of the research was to capture a holistic view of cultural teaching within English language lessons in Slovakia. It offers a naturalistic inquiry through the methods of observation, interview and documentary analysis and provides opportunities to extract the experiences of complex teaching and learning environments. With the use of these three methods (triangulation) different elements of one phenomenon can be explored, inter-related and combined into a coherent, convincing and relevant explanation and argument.

While qualitative research in educational settings is quite a resent phenomenon, it has a long and rich history in anthropology and sociology. Hatch (2002) states that as early as the 1950s scholars (e.g. Jackson, Wolcott, Henry, Spindlers) had started to write about the efficiency of applying qualitative methods to understanding the special social contexts of schools and schooling. It was in the 1970s that the qualitative work began to gain importance as a legitimate form of educational research. Subsequently a number of journals became devoted to publishing qualitative studies while the mainstream journals also began to publish qualitative studies. Qualitative research in education is becoming more and more prominent especially in English speaking countries and it is an equal form of research to quantitative research. They can work well together and can be combined in individual research. Nowadays, qualitative studies are published by the world's leading educational journals. In 1998 Gavora stated that qualitative observation studies in Slovakia were far from sufficient and optimal and now 15 years later the situation of qualitative studies is only slowly changing. The educational system in Slovakia is under the process of reform, many new trends are being implemented into the teaching processes. There is a need to document these changes, as well as their implementation and their impact on education, and my aim is to record at least some of these changes and situations.

3.2. Research paradigm

Hatch (2002) proposes five types of qualitative research paradigm: positivist, post-positivist, constructivist, critical/feminist, poststructuralist, and recommends researchers to find the paradigm framework suitable for their research. This research is mostly concerned with the constructivist paradigm, which is most closely connected with the methodological approach of naturalistic inquiries. The ontology (nature of reality) is concerned with the assumption that absolute realities in the world are unknowable, and the objects of inquiry are individual perspectives or constructions of reality. Constructivists state that there exist multiple realities, which are unique because they are constructed by individuals who experience the world from their own perspectives. Concerning the epistemology (what can be known), it follows that individual constructions of reality compose the knowledge of interest and knowledge is not objective, it is symbolically constructed. Understandings of the world are based on conventions. Naturalistic qualitative methods are used by constructivists, such as interviews and observations in natural settings. Knowledge produced within the constructivist paradigm is produced in the form of case studies, rich narratives, interpretations and reconstructions. During the course of this research individual primary school lessons were observed and teachers were interviewed about the implementation of cultural elements in their English lessons. I expect both lessons and interviews to be quite unique and individual, depending on teachers' understandings and interpretations of cultural teaching within English lessons. The final product is in the form of interpretations.

3.3. Document analysis

According to Cohen, Manion, Morrison (2007) and Flick (2010) documents are standardized artefacts and most of them have been written for a purpose, such as notes, reports, statistics, policy documents, letters, expert opinions, newspaper articles, archives, etc. If we want to understand the nature of documents, we have to move away from considering them as static and pre-defined artefacts. Documents are composed of two dimensions: the authorship and the access to the documents. The authorship can be divided into personal and official documents (official and private). Access to documents can be closed (medical records – documents are not accessible), restricted (judicial records – access is limited to specific professionals), open archival (everyone can have access, but only in a specific archive), open (documents are published and accessible to any interested party). The good quality documents for research must be authentic (genuine and of unquestionable origin), credible (documents must be accurate, the producer must be reliable), representative (whether it is a typical record of the kind), and meaningful (if the documents are clear and comprehensible with the meaning for the reader).

When we decide to use documents in research, we should see them as a means for communication. This means that we should ask ourselves: Who has produced these documents, for which purpose, and for whom? Are the documents produced, used for specific practical purposes? Many documents have been written by skilled professionals and may contain valuable information. The advantage of using documents for analysis is little or no reactivity on the part of the writer, especially if it is not written with the intention of being the research data. To analyse documents we use unobtrusive methods and the outcomes can provide a new and unfiltered perspective on the field and its processes. Documents tend to be factual and another attraction of documents is their availability, often at a low cost. Certain difficulties can arise when analysing documents might be biased and selective. As a stand-alone method, it sometimes provides a limited approach to experiences. In qualitative research, document analysis is best used as a complementary strategy to other methods, such as interviews or observations (Cohen, Manion, Morrison, 2007, Flick 2010).

The methods of coding and categorizing could be applied to process the research data. In this research open coding was applied to document analysis, which expresses data in the form of concepts. This procedure helps to elaborate a deeper understanding of the text. Data are first segmented and then categorized by grouping them around phenomena discovered in the data. Codes should represent the content of each category and should become an aid for referencing the categories. The result should be a list of the codes and categories attached to the text. The aim and the end point of coding is theoretical saturation. All the coding and analysis should be based on constant comparison between materials. However, there might be a problem with open coding because of the potential unlimited number of options for coding and comparisons. That is the reason why there is a need to build a list of priorities and decide which codes should be elaborated further, which codes appear less instructive and which codes could be left out with respect to the research questions (Flick 2010).

This research analysed three various documents concerning the cultural contents recommended for English language lessons at a primary school level. The primary document for the analysis and comparison is the Common European Framework for Languages: Learning, Teaching, Assessment (CEFR, 2001). The two other documents are the Slovak curricular documents for teaching English at primary school level. The A1 language level was chosen from the CEFR- this represents the end of the fifth year of primary schools in Slovakia (age 11). The two Slovak curricular documents, which were chosen for this research consist of the pre-reform English curriculum for primary school level, which was created in 2001 and which was also based on the CEFR, and the current Slovak national curriculum for the English language for ISCED 1 level (2011), which was also based on the CEFR. The plan was to compare both Slovak curricular documents with the CEFR, and with each other, in order to see if there was a shift in the latest documents regarding the cultural contents with the reference to the CEFR. I wanted to find out to what extend the pre-reform curriculum and the current national curriculum reflect the CEFR concerning the implementation of cultural teaching within English language education.

3.4. Observation

The method of observation was also chosen for this research, because it is the most natural research method, as it offers an opportunity to gather "life" data from naturally occurring situations. The researcher works with first-hand (direct) information rather than second-hand accounts. The method of observation has a unique strength in potential authenticity and validity of the data (Cohen, Manion, Morrison, 2007). Observational techniques (both participant and non-participant) are extensively used in qualitative research. There are several types of participation in observation. The "complete participant" is a researcher who takes on an insider role in the studied group, but is not known to be a researcher. The "observer-as-participant" is known to the group as a researcher, but has limited contact with the group. The "participant-as-observer" is known to the group and has access to elements of social life, records and notes of the participants. With the "complete observer" participants do not know that they are being observed (covert observation).

The "observer-as-participant" form of observation was chosen for this research. In this type of observation the researcher is more detached, where objectivity and distance are key characteristics. The observer is known as a researcher to the group, but has less extensive contact with the group. The risk here is the reactivity of the participants, which means that they might alter their behaviour when they know they are being observed (try harder, are more anxious, behave better or worse). The aim of this research was to observe two or three lessons taught by approximately 30 English teachers at primary schools in Slovakia during one school semester. All the teachers were informed beforehand that the aim of the research was to observe cultural aspects in teaching English at primary schools in Slovakia. All the teachers were asked to include something they consider as "cultural aspects" (which they normally do) in the observed lessons (the content and the amount were left to the teachers' choices).

Observation could be performed directly or indirectly. Gavora (1998) recommended to combine direct and indirect observation. Both, direct and indirect types of observation were planned for this research - to observe the lessons directly to get the information first hand, and to make the video recordings (indirect observation) of the lessons for further references. The teachers felt very uneasy with having their lessons recorded and so consent to record the lessons was not given. The direct observation was carried out in the natural settings of primary schools, where the observer (the author) was placed in the back of the classroom so as not to disturb the lessons.

The semi-structured scheme was created for my "observer-as-participant" research. The constant comparison technique was used to collect data. The hypothesis was not set. During the research process, I collected data, categorized them, focused on common features, differences and relationships between them. Some categories were refined, unsuitable categories were excluded and new categories were added in. First of all, an observation scheme was prepared with the main categories (where the researcher has an agenda of issues in a less systematic order than in structured observation). These categories just set the main areas of interest and I took notes which were relevant for the research. But unlike structured observation, exact categories were not set, where frequency or incidents of elements would be marked. However, systematization of the categories (also in semi-structured observation) increases the reliability of the data. From unstructured observation the technique of field notes was applied, where chronological and detailed notes of the lessons were written down (physical setting, people in the situation, activities, events, time, goals, feelings etc.). The observation scheme categories focused on the amount and extent of cultural teaching (how much time was spent on cultural teaching), integration of cultural teaching (if the cultural teaching was integrated with the language teaching, or taught separately), the content of cultural teaching (whether the teachers focused more on the visible culture, or the invisible culture), competences being developed by cultural teaching (general, linguistic, sociolinguistic, pragmatic, paralinguistic), skills being developed by cultural teaching (speaking, reading, listening, writing), critical thinking being developed by cultural teaching, materials used for cultural teaching, methods used for cultural teaching and most importantly the aim of cultural teaching.

For the data processing, the grounded theory of coding was applied, where the data are broken down, conceptualized, and put back together in new ways. The first step in coding is to develop and unfold an understanding of the issues (substantive sampling - words and concepts). Then the relationships among the codes (causes, contexts, consequences and conditions) are searched for. This is called theoretical sampling. It can go from causes to phenomena and to consequences (What are the causes of the phenomena and what are the consequences?). The findings have to be addressed to the empirical materials and answers provided by coding and comparison. The process of grounded theory is based on a great deal of intuition in the early decisions and becomes more systematic in its development. The end point of coding is theoretical saturation, which means that there are no more new properties and the continuous coding does not lead to new theoretical insights. Choosing the right coding methods increases reliability. The way of checking reliability is to compare the interpretation of the researcher with the other data, to improve comparability. The more detailed the research process is in its documentation, the more reliable it is. The aim of grounded theory is to develop a new theory, where there is a lack of theoretical knowledge. The current research fills the gap of the lacking theoretical knowledge concerning the implementation of cultural aspects in English language lessons in primary schools in Slovakia (Gavora, 1998, Cohen, Manion, Morrison, 2007, Flick 2010).

3.5. Interview

A semi-structured interview was also chosen for this research, which is the most commonly used interview technique in qualitative research. An open-ended schedule which could be reordered, digressions and expansions made, new entries included, and further inquiries undertaken, was created by the researcher. With the method of interview, further matters arising from observations could be explored. The method of interview in qualitative research focuses on capturing uniqueness, individuality, subjective facts, informality, etc. The researcher tries to understand and interpret the key features of the participants' statements. The use of natural language is applied to gather and understand qualitative data. The aim is to focus on specific ideas and themes and to elicit descriptions of specific situations and actions, rather than come to generalizations. The questions can be phrased or organized in a direct or indirect form. The direct form might in some sensitive matters appear as too abrupt, and that is why the researcher might choose an indirect approach. From the answers, the interviewer could make deductions about the teachers' opinions and beliefs. In this case the teachers felt very uneasy about saying how good their own intercultural communicative competencies were and what they knew about what cultural aspects should be included in the language lessons (Cohen, Manion, Morrison, 2007, Flick 2010). I tried to find out these matters indirectly by giving them hints and asking them about the specific content of their teaching (by giving them themes of cultural content, but asking them to give examples of what they normally do for each theme).

The aim of the interview method in my project was to find out the English teachers' experiences, self-reflecting competences, preferences, the content of cultural teaching in their lessons, but also where the teachers get their guidance for cultural teaching from and which aspects of the language they pay the most attention to. All the observed teachers (30) and also other English teachers (21) were interviewed. The other English teachers were teachers from all around Slovakia that I met at conferences and meetings, and I used the opportunity to interview them. The interview method was implemented ethically; interviewees were assured of the confidential nature of the process and the earnest and honest approach of the study. Thus they were put at ease and informed that the interview may be to their advantage in terms of improving the teaching of the English language at primary school level in Slovakia.

The results of the interviews can be validated by comparing them with other results. The interviewer can ensure validity by being neutral, avoiding having strong opinions and expectations, and developing a non-threatening, friendly rapport with the interviewee based on mutual trust and respect. Factors which affect the validity of interviews are: authenticity, honesty, depth of response, richness of response, and commitment to the interviewee. Reliability is ensured through implementing a highly structured, consistent interview with the same sequence of words and questions for each respondent, and through using closed questions. In this research, I decided on opting for a semi-structured interview where a degree of reliability is ensured by semi-structured questions. Also an opportunity for interviewees to express themselves is provided in the open-ended questions (Cohen,

Manion, Morrison, 2007, Flick 2010). Also Silverman (2006) advises using open-ended questions, as they are flexible, and they enable respondents to express their views and opinions about the situation. If the interviewer is detached and direct throughout, the interview process can perceived to be unfriendly and interrogative and so this can have a negative impact on the validity of the research.

The analysis of the qualitative data from the interviews was carried out by categorising and coding. The data analyses are inevitably open to interpretation, they are more of a reflexive, reactive interaction between the researcher and the data (interpretations of social encounters). Coding can be understood as the translation of question responses and respondent information to specific categories for the purposes of analysis. It is the process of crediting a category label to a piece of data (categories could be decided in advance or as a response to the collected data) (Cohen, Manion, Morrison, 2007, Flick 2010).

3.6. Reliability and validity

Qualitative research, in this case also should be holistic, should record multiple interpretations of, intentions in and meanings given to situations and events. Reliability here can be defined as dependability and this was ensured during the course of this research through the use of triangulation, prolonged engagement in the field and persistent observation. The rules of reliability for quantitative research cannot be applied to qualitative research (Cohen, Manion, Morrison, 2007, Flick 2010). Naturalistic study cannot be replicated the same way in quantitative research, but some similarities exist between quantitative and qualitative research and these include the following: the status position of the researcher, the choice of informant/respondents, the methods of data collection and analysis, situations and conditions. Reliability is regarded as an agreeableness between what the researcher records as data and what actually occurs in the natural setting that is being researched (a degree of accuracy and comprehensiveness of coverage). Reliability in qualitative research includes faithfulness to real life, authenticity, comprehensiveness, detail, honesty, depth of response and meaningfulness to the respondents. Data from documents are objective data, which ensure reliability of the findings. The data collected from observation and interviews are so extensive that they trustfully offer authentic material faithful to real life, with a lot of detail and depth. During the course of the research, I was neutral, consistent and honest. By managing all these intentions, reliability of the current research was provided.

The issue of validity in qualitative research can be addressed through honesty, the depth, richness and scope of the data, the extent of triangulation, objectivity of the researcher, prolonged engagement in the field, persistent observation, etc. Only those qualities were chosen, which are connected with the current type of research, and which were applied to this project (Lincoln, Guba, 1985). Generalizability in naturalistic research is interpreted as comparability and transferability, whether it is possible to assess the typicality of a situation (participants and settings), to identify possible comparison groups, and to indicate how data might translate into different settings (Cohen, Manion, Morrison, 2007). Lincoln and Guba (1985) suggest that the researchers' task is to provide sufficiently rich data for the readers and users of the research to determine whether transferability is possible. Validity can be also ensured by choosing an appropriate time scale, adequate resources for the required research, an appropriate methodology for answering the research questions, appropriate instrumentation for gathering the data, an appropriate sample, reducing "halo" and "horns" effects, avoiding selective use of data, avoiding subjective interpretation of data, making claims which are sustainable by the data, avoiding inaccurate or wrong reporting of data, and ensuring that the research questions are answered (Cohen, Manion, Morrison, 2007). All the mentioned issues were considered throughout the course of the research to ensure validity of the project. In this research, an insight is provided into the issue of implementing cultural aspects in English language teaching, with the aim of addressing professionals concerned with teaching English (to identify the issue, to recognize the problems, compare experiences, transfer the findings to their circumstances and possibly to attempt to improve the issues). The objective of this research is to offer an insight which would be easily transferable to different settings.

A triangulation of methods is used to maximise the validity of the data. Triangulation attempts to map out, or explain more fully, the richness and complexity of situations by studying them from more than one standpoint. The researcher takes different perspectives on an issue in order to answer the research questions. The whole picture is gained by combining observation with document analyses and interviews. Individually, each research method provides only a limited view of the complexity of situations, but by combining and comparing a holistic view is acquired. In triangulation there are three types of results: converging results, complementary results and contradictions. If research using the different methods ends up with convergent results, it means that one method would have been enough to use. It is more interesting and justifiable, when the results are either complementary or contradictory. When these appeared in the current research, the author's responsibility was to look for a theoretical explanation of where these differences came from (Cohen, Manion, Morrison, 2007, Flick 2010).

3.7. Ethics

Participants in this project were included on the basis of informed consent, and on a voluntary basis with rights to withdraw at any time. Copies of the report are available to the participants. I, the researcher declare that I withheld the participants names or other identifying characteristics and that I did not use the data in any way which would publicly identify the schools.

3.8. Sampling

Sampling in the research is based on the most typical form of selecting material in qualitative research –theoretical sampling. Theoretical sampling is a more concrete strategy and is closer to everyday life than classical sampling. The process of data collection is controlled by the emerging theory and the researcher decides along the way on what additional data to collect, and where to find it. The exact sample size is not known in advance and sampling is finished when theoretical saturation is reached. The strategy of theoretical sampling also refers to data triangulation, in which the integration of various data sources is used. Theoretical sampling requires the researcher to have sufficient data to be able to generate the theory, to create a theoretical explanation of what is happening in the situation. The samples might be fixed or limited by the number of people to whom one has access, but the researcher needs to keep the "door open" for going back in order to gather further data for theoretical saturation. Samples of people are selected as per the researcher's needs to address specific issues, so the question is not only who to sample, but also what to sample. Also texts and documents may be sampled by theoretical sampling.

The aim of the research was to gain an insight into how cultural aspects are implemented in English language lessons in primary schools in Slovakia. The plan was to develop a theoretical explanation of what is the real situation of English teaching in Slovakia. The methods of observation, interview and document analysis were used for the data collection. The sample for observation included 50 lessons (between one and three lessons conducted by 30 English teachers) from primary schools in the Nitra region in Slovakia. All the observed teachers (30) plus additional 21 English teachers from all around Slovakia were interviewed. The documentary sampling included the Common European Framework of Reference for Languages, the pre-reform curriculum and the new national curriculum.

3.9. Research subjects

For conducting the observation a sample of 30 English language teachers from the Nitra region was gathered. Volunteer sampling was applied for this research as not many schools and teachers were willing to cooperate in this study. The average length of teaching experience of the observed teachers was 11 years (15 teachers had up to 5 years of experience, 6 teachers had up to 10 years of experience, 4 teachers had up to 15 years of experience and 5 teachers had up to 25 years of experience). However, the length of teaching experience did not equate with the length of English teaching experience, which is an understandable fact due to our historical development. The average length of English teaching experience was 9 years (17 teachers had up to 5 years of experience, 5 teachers had up to 10 years of experience, 4 teachers had up to 15 years and 4 teachers had up to 25 years of experience). An interesting fact was that out of 30 observed teachers there was only 1 male teacher and 29 female teachers.

Interviews were conducted with all observed teachers (30) plus the additional 21 teachers who volunteered to be consulted. The additional teachers came from villages and towns from diverse locations across the country (e.g. Trenčín, Levice, Rožňava, Mlynky, Prievidza, Handlová, Trnava, Dubnica nad Váhom, Mankovce, etc.) and I met them at conferences and various occasions.

The researcher conducting observations and interviews is a qualified PhD lecturer of Methodology of teaching English at the Department of Language Pedagogy and Intercultural Studies at the Faculty of Education Constantine the Philosopher University in Nitra. She is an experienced teacher and researcher with rich intercultural experiences from many years of living in other countries. The researcher has been teaching courses on the culture of English-speaking countries, intercultural communication, sociolinguistics and phonetics and phonology at the Department of Language Pedagogy and Intercultural Studies.

3.10. Stages in research

The whole research lasted for two years. Background literature and previous works were studied and a theoretical framework was constructed in the early stages of 2011. In the second quarter of 2011 methodological procedures and samples were chosen and research questions were generated. Document analyses by categorising and coding were undertaken in the third quarter of 2011. Observation of English language lessons and interviews with teachers lasted for approximately 9 months from the end of 2011 until the first half of 2012. Analyses by categorizing and coding of the collected data and triangulating the outcomes of the three methods were conducted in the second half of 2012.

4. Research analyses

4.1. Document analyses

In this project, one of the aims was to analyse and compare three various documents concerning the cultural aspects recommended for teaching English at a primary school level. The documents for the analyses and comparisons were: the Common European Framework for Languages: Learning, Teaching, Assessment A1 level (CERF, 2001), the Slovak pre-reform English curriculum for the primary school level (2001) and the current Slovak national curriculum for the English language ISCED 1 (2011). Slovak education, including foreign language education, is currently going through a curricular reform. The CEFR provides a basis for the elaboration of language curriculum guidelines, syllabi, textbooks, etc. across Europe. Also both Slovak curricular documents chosen for the analyses were based on the CEFR. The CEFR covers the cultural contexts in which languages are set and promotes the intercultural development of the learners. It recommends a combination of linguistic and cultural competences in order to develop socio-cultural knowledge, intercultural awareness, intercultural skills and know-how. From the beginning of the pupils' education, the intercultural approach is especially important, as it promotes the favourable development of their personalities, attitudes towards other languages and cultures, and a sense of identity associate with the enriching experience of otherness in language and culture. This is also why the primary school level was chosen for this research, as it is important to include the intercultural approach in foreign language education from a very early age. Furthermore, during the time of curricular reform, there is a great justification for the comparison of the curricular documents.

4.1.1. CEFR

The A1 level in the CEFR is also called the Breakthrough level, which is the first stage of becoming the basic user. The general descript for the CEFR A1 level (2001, p. 24) states that the learner: "can understand and use familiar everyday expressions and very basic phrases aimed at the satisfaction of needs of a concrete type. Can introduce him/herself and others and can ask and answer questions about personal details such as where he/she lives, people he/she knows and things he/she has. Can interact in a simple way provided the other person talks slowly and clearly and is prepared to help". The other descriptors set the standard for the basic skills, such as listening, reading, speaking and writing. When listening (CEFR 2001, p. 26), the learners should be able to recognize familiar words, basic phrases concerning themselves, family and concrete surroundings. When reading (ibid.), a learner should be able to understand familiar names, words, simple sentences, notices, posters and catalogues. When speaking (ibid.), a learner should be able to interact in a simple way, repeat, rephrase things, ask and answer simple questions, describe where he/she lives and people they know. When writing (ibid.), a learner should be able to write a simple short postcard, holiday greeting, or fill in forms with personal details. The other descriptors deal with the linguistic range (p. 110), vocabulary range (p. 112), grammatical (p. 114), phonological (p. 117), orthographic (p. 118) accuracy and sociolinguistic appropriateness (p. 122). Also the description of "real life" tasks is given for the A1 level. The learner reaching the breakthrough level (CEFR 2001, p. 31) should be able to make simple purchases (using pointing and gestures), ask and tell which day it is, the time of day and date, use basic greetings, say yes, no, excuse me, please, thank you, sorry, fill-in uncomplicated forms with personal details and write a short simple postcard. The last mentioned descriptors are concerned with intercultural communication.

Consequently, the base document chosen for this analysis and comparisons is the Common European Framework for Languages: Learning, Teaching, Assessment (CEFR, 2001). From the CEFR, the A1 level was selected, which represents the end of the fifth year of primary schools in Slovakia (age 11). The Slovak curricular documents are also represented by the same age category, the end of the primary school level. The aim was to analyse and compare the old (pre-reform) and new (current) Slovak curricula with the CEFR, whether the Slovak curricula follow the recommendations of the CEFR considering the implementation of cultural aspects into English language teaching. The study also compared the two Slovak curricula, to see whether there was a positive shift from the old to the new documents concerning the implementation of cultural teaching within English language education.

The intercultural concept in the CEFR is similar to Byram's (1997) model of ICC (see p. 31–33). He developed a model for foreign language teachers on how to teach and assess ICC. The model declares that the linguistic, sociolinguistic, discourse and intercultural competences are the dimensions of the ICC. Byram (ibid.) names the factors influencing intercultural communicative competence: attitudes, knowledge, skills of interpreting and relating, skills of discovery and interaction and critical cultural awareness.

The CEFR divides competences into "general competences" and "communicative language competences". General competences consist of "knowledge", "skills", "existential competence" and "ability to learn". Communicative language competences comprise of "linguistic", "sociolinguistic" and "pragmatic" components. Development of ICC is one of the main priorities of foreign language teaching, however the CEFR does not elaborate on the development of ICC for each level of proficiency. The CEFR only describes the competences in general, and the aspects of ICC are only included in individual competences and therefore the connection with ICC is not immediately obvious. This is why I have excerpted them from the CEFR and summarised general and communicative competences connected to culture and created clear diagrams, which can serve as basis for cultural teaching.

In the component of knowledge the empirical knowledge relating to day-to-day living, shared values and beliefs of social groups is considered to be essential to intercultural communication. Existential competence is considered to be culture-related as it includes the sum of personal characteristics, personality traits, attitudes, self-image and one's view of others. These factors are the product of acculturation and can be modified. Existential competence refers to intercultural perceptions and relations (what can be considered as friendliness in one culture might be perceived as offence in another culture). Sociolinguistic competences refer to the socio-cultural conditions of language use (rules of politeness, norms relating to relations between generations, sexes, classes and social groups). The sociolinguistic component affects all communication between representatives of different cultures. Pragmatic competences are concerned with the functional use of the language. The cultural component is very important here, as the ability to use the language suitably depends not only on linguistic competences, but also on the cultural environments in which the interactions are constructed. "Non-verbal communication" must not be forgotten as an important part of intercultural communication. Paralinguistic features, such as gestures, facial expressions, eye contact, body contact, proxemics; extra-linguistic speech sounds for expressing silence, happiness, disgust, approval, disapproval etc.; and prosodic features such as loudness, pitch of the voice are very delicate features in intercultural communication. They vary from culture to culture and can cause great misunderstandings if perceived or performed inappropriately. The following diagrams summarise the cultural aspects in connection with the general and communicative competences.

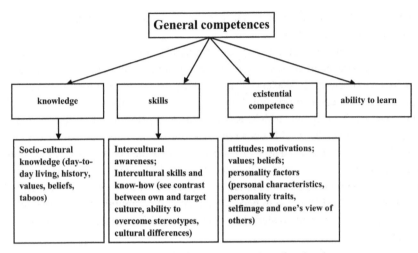

Figure 3: *General competences connected with culture*

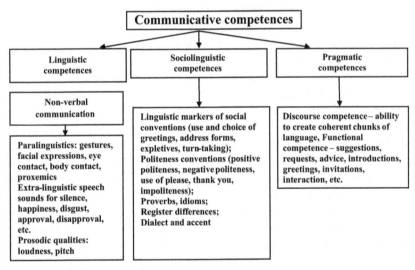

Figure 4: *Communicative competences connected with culture*

For the analysis of the curricular documents I created categories and codes based on figures 3 and 4. The figures were created for the purposes of analysing cultural contents by summarizing cultural aspects from the CEFR. Additionally, categories and codes for recommended materials, methods and techniques were created. Not all the categories or codes were specified in the descriptors for each level of language proficiency. As it was mentioned above, the descriptors dealt more with setting the standards for reading, speaking, writing and listening skills, vocabulary, grammar, phonological, orthographic accuracy rather than aspects concerning ICC. However, there were a few descriptors which in theory deal with ICC. One of them is the descriptor for sociolinguistic appropriateness for the A1 level, which stated that the learner should be able to establish basic social contact by using the simplest everyday polite forms of greetings and farewells, introductions, saying please, thank you, sorry, etc. The other one was mentioned above as the descriptor for "real life" tasks (making simple purchases, asking and saying what time, day and date it is, using basic greetings, saying yes, no, excuse me, please, thank you, sorry, filling-in uncomplicated forms with personal details, writing a short simple postcard). These categories and codes are a result of a laborious excerption of specific cultural contents, which are not obvious and easily obtainable for language teachers, who want to get guidelines for their cultural teaching.

It is recommended by many specialists and also CEFR that the development of ICC should be started at a very early age. As the CEFR does not specify the ICC exactly, it is difficult for the curricula implementers to decide which cultural aspects should be included in the language teaching for each level of proficiency. The following table of categories and codes could serve as the basis of contents for cultural teaching.

Categories	Code Nr.	Codes	Examples
Sociolinguistic competences	1	greetings, addressing	upon arrival, leaving, introduction, formal, informal, familiar
	2	use of exclamations	Dear, dear! My God! Bloody Hell!
	3	positive politeness	admiration, hospitality, affection, showing interest,
	4	negative politeness	apologizing, expressing regret, avoiding direct orders
	5	appropriate use of	please, thank you
	6	impoliteness	bluntness, dislike, anger, impatience, complaints
	7	proverbs, idioms	sealed lips, smacking lips

Categories	Code Nr.	Codes	Examples
	8	register (language use in different contexts) (p. 120)	formal (May I come in, please?), neutral (Shall we begin?), informal (Right. Can we start?), familiar (O.K. Let's get going), intimate (Ready dear?)
	9	dialect, accent (p. 121)	social class, regional differences, ethnicity
Pragmatic competences	10	suasion (advising, persuading, urging) (p. 126)	suggestions, asking for help, requests, warnings, advice, invitations, encouragement
	11	socialising (p. 126)	attracting attention, toasting, greetings
	12	interaction patterns (127)	turn taking
Non-verbal communication	13	body language (p. 89)	gestures, facial expressions, posture, eye contact, body contact, proxemics
	14	extra linguistic speech sounds (p. 89)	for silence, approval, disapproval, disgust
	15	prosodic qualities (p. 89)	loudness, pitch
Socio-cultural knowledge	16	everyday living (p. 102)	food and drink, meal times, table manners, public holidays, leisure activities,
	17	living conditions (p. 102)	housing, welfare, living standards
	18	interpersonal relations (p. 102)	class structure, family structure, relations between generations, sexes, etc.
	19	values, beliefs, attitudes, people, country (p. 103)	institutions, social change, history, states, politics, religion, humour, national identity, arts, etc.
	20	social conventions (p. 103)	dress, presents, punctuality
	21	ritual behaviour (p. 103)	festivals, celebrations, traditions, weddings, funerals

Categories	Code Nr.	Codes	Examples
Recommended materials	22	authentic texts	books, newspapers, magazines, public signs, notices, leaflets, packaging
	23	authentic language (p. 56, 143, 148, 154)	native speakers, radio, TV, media
	24	special books (p. 148)	encyclopaedias, etc.
	25	computers (p. 143)	games, emails, internet
Recommended methods and techniques	26	role-plays, games, simulations (p. 56, 148)	
	27	discussions, negotiations (p. 145, 148)	
	28	explanations, illustrations (p. 145, 148)	
	29	creating portfolio (p. 175)	Language biography including more informal experiences with language and other cultures

Table 2:   Main categories and codes based on CEFR

4.1.2. Slovak curriculum for the English language for primary school level (2001)

Before the new concept for teaching English was introduced in 2007, foreign language teaching at primary school level was considered only as an alternative form of education, for which only the most talented children should be carefully chosen. In 2001 a curriculum for teaching English at a primary school level was introduced (accredited by the Ministry of Education, Act 3276/2000–41, valid from 1st September 2001). This curriculum was also based on the Common European Framework of Reference for languages. The authors of the curriculum emphasised the importance of early language teaching, as it opens new horizon for culture varieties, diminishes ethnocentric tendencies, helps to develop tolerance towards other cultures and reflect upon one's own language and culture. One of the main aims was to develop the learners' interest in other languages and cultures, so that they would be interested in the outside world and consequently be able to develop an increased level of confidence and understanding.

The Curriculum was divided to each school year separately (year one, year two, year three and year four), in other words each year had its own specific curriculum. The content of the curriculum was also divided into the various subjects of interest (my school, my family, clothes, seasons, means of transport, etc.) vocabulary, grammar, pronunciation tips, reading, listening, speaking and writing skills and intercultural learning. All the aspects were clearly divided into each school year, but the drawback was that the target language level was not set (as it is in the CEFR).

As a result of the research being focused on the A1 level according to the CEFR, each school year was not analysed separately, but instead the whole curriculum was analysed for primary school education. Applying the defined system of categories and codes, the following findings are summarized in the accompanying table:

Categories	Code Nr.	Codes	Occurrence in various contexts	Examples
Sociolinguistic competences	1	greetings, addressing	5	greetings, addressing people in oral interaction, in written communication, differences between Slovak and English "you", How are you?
	2	use of exclamations	0	
	3	positive politeness	5	Would you like some/a..? Here you are. Do you like? Thank you. Help yourself. I like it. It's delicious.
	4	negative politeness	2	Apologizing
	5	appropriate use of	1	please, thank you
	6	impoliteness	1	It's horrible. Expressing dislikes (I don't like...)
	7	proverbs, idioms	0	
	8	register (language use in different contexts) (p. 120)	0	
	9	dialect, accent (p. 121)	0	

Categories	Code Nr.	Codes	Occurrence in various contexts	Examples
Pragmatic compe-tences	10	suasion (advising, persuading, urging) (p. 126)	0	
	11	socialising (p. 126)	2	addressing in letters, writing letters and greeting cards, postcards
	12	interaction patterns (127)	0	
Non-verbal commu-nication	13	body language (p. 89)	0	
	14	extra linguistic speech sounds (p. 89)	0	
	15	prosodic qualities (p. 89)	0	
Socio-cultural knowledge	16	everyday living (p. 102)	3	food, clothes, transport
	17	living conditions (p. 102)	0	
	18	interpersonal relations (p. 102)	1	women's surnames (Slovak vs. English equivalent)
	19	people, country (p. 103)	5	places in own and target country, English schools, uniforms, information about English speaking countries, capital cities: London, Washington, currencies: dollar, pound
	20	social conventions (p. 103)	0	
	21	ritual behaviour (p. 103)	5	Christmas, Easter, Halloween, New Year, birthdays, celebrations, traditions, festivals

Categories	Code Nr.	Codes	Occurrence in various contexts	Examples
Recomm-ended materials	22	authentic texts	0	
	23	authentic language (p. 56, 143, 148, 154)	0	
	24	special books (p. 148)	0	
	25	computers (p. 143	0	
Recomm-ended methods and techniques	26	role-plays, games, simulations (p. 56, 148)	0	
	27	discussions, negotiations (p. 145, 148)	0	
	28	explanations, illustrations (p. 145, 148)	0	
	29	creating portfolio (p. 175)	0	

Table 3:   Categories and codes present in the pre-reform curriculum

From the above table it can be seen, that only 10 codes were mentioned in the curriculum. The remaining 19 codes were not included.

The greatest importance was given to the following cultural aspects, which occurred in the curriculum in five various places. These aspects were represented by these codes: code number 1 "greetings, addressing", number 3 "positive politeness", number 19 "people, country" and number 21 "ritual behaviour". Code number 1 "greetings, addressing" was mentioned only generally with a few examples (How are you? differences between Slovak and English "you"), which is insufficient. A wider range of examples of greetings and the different ways of addressing people would be more suitable. Code number 3 "positive politeness" was better represented by examples such as: Would you like some/a…?; Here you are.; Do you like?; Thank you.; Help yourself.; I like it.; It's delicious. Codes 1 and 3 develop the sociolinguistic competences. Code number 19 "people, country" was sufficient enough for this level of language proficiency (knowledge on places, English schools, uniforms, information about English speaking countries, capital cities: London, Washington and currencies: dollar, pound). Code number 21 "ritual behaviour" included celebrations, festivals and traditions (Christmas, Easter, Halloween, New Year, birthdays), which is considered as adequate. Code numbers 19 and 21 belong to the category of socio-cultural knowledge and they were very well represented in the curriculum.

The following codes were mentioned three times, twice or once. Code number 16 "everyday living" belongs to the socio-cultural knowledge category and was illustrated by learning about food, clothes and transport. However there was no more explanation for what should be included in these topics and some tips for teachers should be included. Code number 4 "negative politeness" belongs to the sociolinguistic competence and was mentioned twice, but only that pupils should be able to apologize, but no examples of apologies which would be useful were given. Code number 11 "socialising" belongs to the pragmatic competence and was also mentioned twice and focused on how to address people in letters, how to write letters, greeting cards and postcards. This level of competence is appropriate for the A1 language proficiency. Code number 5 "appropriate use of thank you and please" belongs to the sociolinguistic competence and it was mentioned once without any explanation or suggestion about what the appropriate use of these phrases are. The differences in the use of "please and thank you" between Slovak and English are considerable and they require more attention. Code number 6 "impoliteness" belongs to the sociolinguistic competence and was mentioned once with the way of expressing dislikes (I don't like…, It's horrible), which should be sufficient enough. Code number 18 "interpersonal relations" belongs to the socio-cultural knowledge category and was represented by introducing the differences between women's surnames (Slovak vs. English equivalent), which is adequate for this level.

19 codes were never mentioned in the curriculum, which is almost twice as many as those which were included (10). Not all the codes have equal importance or weight, but codes such as number 10 (advising, persuading), number 13 (body language), 17 (living conditions), 22–25 (materials) and 26–29 (methods and techniques) should be included with basic information and tips. Even some of the codes which have been included are insufficiently covered. For example code number 1 (greetings) and code number 5 (appropriate use of please and thank you) should require more attention, as the appropriate phrases belong to the basic knowledge, which every learner acquires right at the beginning of language learning. Over all, the following main categories such as sociolinguistic competences,

pragmatic competences and socio-cultural knowledge were included in the curriculum, however non-verbal communication and materials and methods for teaching culture were not even mentioned.

4.1.3. Slovak national curriculum for the English language ISCED 1 (2011)

A new concept for foreign language teaching at primary and secondary schools in Slovakia was accredited by the government of the Slovak Republic on 12th September 2007 (767/2007). The aim of the curricular reform was to standardise English language teaching in all schools in Slovakia and to improve the standards of foreign language education. The priority was to provide effective foreign language education for children from a very early age, as young children already begin to form key attitudes towards other languages and cultures, which may remain deep seated in later life. As a consequence, compulsory foreign language education has been brought forward to the third year of primary school education. The plan of the language reform was to bring the accredited changes into practice at the earliest by the school year 2008/2009, or in the school year 2009/2010 (Koncepcia vyučovania cudzích jazykov v základných a stredných školách, 2007, p. 34). The insufficient number of qualified foreign language teachers at primary school level was a problem and so the plan was to recruit a greater number of qualified foreign language teachers within three years (Koncepcia..., 2007, p. 24). The transition period should last until the school years 2017–2019 at the latest. After 2019 all the schools will have to provide the teaching of foreign languages in correspondence with the reformed concept of foreign language education (Koncepcia..., 2007, p. 21). Based on the new concept of foreign language education, at least two foreign languages should be learned by each pupil in Slovakia. The first foreign language should be taught from the third year (8 year old pupils) of primary school and the second foreign language should be taught from the fifth year (10 year old pupils) of primary school. Also the number of language lessons has increased. Levels of language proficiency are set according to the CEFR for each level of education. On 1st February 2011 the Slovak Parliament passed an amendment to the School Act (245/2008) about the English language becoming a compulsory foreign language taught in schools.

Even though the plan of the reform was to bring the accredited changes into practice during the school year 2008/2009 (or 2009/2010), the national curriculum for the English language was only published in May 2011. Primary schools were to make their own school curricula based on the national curriculum, which was truly impossible with the national curriculum coming three years late. This is quite an important fact showing faults in the curricular reform.

Nevertheless, the next step of this analysis was to focus on the current national curriculum for the English language at primary school level. The analyses of the current national curriculum were also based on the CEFR A1 proficiency level. However, the A1 level corresponds with the end of the fifth year of primary school (first year of the lower secondary education) and the level for primary education (the end of the fourth year) is slightly modified in the national curriculum to the A1.1 level. The national curriculum is not divided into individual school years, only the target level A1.1 is described. The national curriculum describes the following aims and competences.

General aims cover various aspects concerning the acquisition of a foreign language, where the development of intercultural competences is mentioned as one of the aims. Social aims are characterized too generally and they can be applied to any other subject, e.g. cooperation with partners, providing help and encouragement to others, ability to adjust, to accept failure, etc.

General competences are described as competences which are not characteristic for language and they do not correspond with the CEFR. The CEFR describes general competences as knowledge, skills, existential competences and the ability to learn and all of them are portrayed in connection with language including the intercultural issues (see figure 3). The above mentioned important issues are missing in the national curriculum.

Communicative competences mention linguistic competences, sociolinguistic competences (basic social communication, greetings, introduction, thanking) and pragmatic competences (only on the level of combining letters and joining words with conjunctions "and", "or"). These descriptions are considered to be insufficient in comparison with the CEFR (see figure 4). Reference to non-verbal communication is absent (see figure 4).

The curriculum deals further with the description of skills (reading, listening, speaking, writing), and only a few cultural aspects are mentioned. In speaking skills the ability to introduce ourselves, greet somebody, ask how they are, ask and answer questions about everyday life is mentioned. And in the writing skills the ability to write a postcard is included.

A great part of the curriculum is devoted to functions and competences in the English language for the A1 proficiency level. It names and describes 25 different competences for the A1 to B2 levels, which should be based on the CEFR, but are taken from the publication *"Un Referentiel: Textes ET References Niveau B2 Pour Le Francais/Livre - Conseil Europe"* (Beacco, J.-C., Bouquet, S., Porquier, R., 2004).

However, these 25 competences are nowhere to be found in the CEFR. The competences which are included in the curriculum for the A1 level are mentioned: relating with others to a communicative situation (1), listening to and giving information (2), choosing from given possibilities (3), expressing opinion (4), expressing willingness (5), expressing ability (6), expressing feelings (7), expressing expectations and reactions to expectations (8), discussing interests and tastes (9), setting rules and regulations (11), making and responding to offers (14), responding to possible events (15), meeting people for the first time (17), correspondence (18), making a phone call (19), monitoring understanding (24). Some of these competences include the intercultural aspect, which are illustrated and described later.

The last part of the curriculum deals with the topics for communication for the level A1.1+ and suggestions for the development of language skills and the way of evaluating pupils. Fourteen topics are named without any closer description: family and society, home and living, human body, transport, education, humans and nature, hobbies and free time, food, multicultural society, clothes and fashion, sports, shopping, countries, towns and places, ideals). More descriptions, ideas and tips are needed in the curriculum. For better illustration, the occurrence of cultural issues in the curriculum was put in the following table:

Categories	Code Nr.	Codes	Occurrence in various contexts	Examples
Sociolinguistic competences	1	greetings, addressing	4	Introducing oneself (I'm.../My name is...) and others (This is.../ My mother's name is...), responding to introductions (Hello, how are you?), expressing welcome (Welcome. Come in.), greeting by arrival (Hello/ Hi/Good morning/ Good afternoon/ Good evening) and departure (Good night/Goodbye/ Bye-bye/Bye)

Categories	Code Nr.	Codes	Occurrence in various contexts	Examples
	2	use of exclamations	0	
	3	positive politeness	1	Expressing likes: I love…/ I like…,
	4	negative politeness	0	
	5	appropriate use of	2	Thank you. Thanks. That's ok. OK. Yes, please. No, thank you.
	6	impoliteness	1	Dislike (I don't like…)
	7	proverbs, idioms	0	
	8	register (language use in different contexts) (p. 120)	0	
	9	dialect, accent (p. 121)	0	
Pragmatic competences	10	suasion (advising, persuading, urging) (p. 126)	4	Making requests (Speak slowly, Can I go…, please?) responding to requests (Yes. Ok. No, sorry.), suggesting something (Can you..?/Let's play), offering help (Can I help you?), monitoring understanding (Does he understand?/Can you spell your name?/ How do you say it in English?/Can you repeat it please?)
	11	socialising (p. 126)	3	Written greetings, letters (how to start and finish), telephone conversation
	12	interaction patterns (127)	0	
Non-verbal communication	13	body language (p. 89)	0	

Categories	Code Nr.	Codes	Occurrence in various contexts	Examples
	14	extra linguistic speech sounds (p. 89)	0	
	15	prosodic qualities (p. 89)	0	
Socio-cultural knowledge	16	everyday living (p. 102)	0	
	17	living conditions (p. 102)	0	
	18	interpersonal relations (p. 102)	0	
	19	values, beliefs, attitudes, people, country (p. 103)	0	
	20	social conventions (p. 103)	0	
	21	ritual behaviour (p. 103)	1	foreign languages, celebrations, cultures coming together
Recommended materials	22	authentic texts	0	
	23	authentic language (p. 56, 143, 148, 154)	0	
	24	special books (p. 148)	0	
	25	computers (p. 143	0	
Recommended methods and techniques	26	role-plays, games, simulations (p. 56, 148)	0	
	27	discussions, negotiations (p. 145, 148)	0	
	28	explanations, illustrations (p. 145, 148)	0	
	29	creating portfolios (p. 175)	1	Self-evaluating notes, collection of drawings, projects, tests, etc.

Table 4:   Categories and codes present in the current national curriculum

From the above table it is apparent, that only 8 codes were included in the current national curriculum. The remaining 21 codes were not mentioned, which is a numerically similar result as with the pre reform curriculum (see Table. 4), where 10 codes were included and 19 codes were not.

The greatest importance was given to the development of some aspects of the sociolinguistic and pragmatic competences, from which the most frequent codes appeared in four various places. These aspects were represented by these codes: code number 1 "greetings, addressing" and code number 10 "suasion - advising, persuading, urging". Code number 1 "greetings, addressing" was mentioned in the introduction of the curriculum, but mainly in competence number 1 (Relating with others in a communicative situation) and competence number 17 (Meeting people for the first time). This code suggests: introducing oneself (I'm.../My name is...) and others (This is.../ My mother's name is...), responding to introductions (Hello, how are you?), expressing welcome (Welcome. Come in.), greeting by arrival (Hello/Hi/Good morning/ Good afternoon/Good evening) and departure (Good night/Goodbye/Bye-bye/Bye). Code number 1 "greetings, addressing" was well and sufficiently represented with the aim of developing the sociolinguistic competence. Code number 10 "suasion - advising, persuading, urging" was present in competence number 14 (Making and responding to offers) and competence number 24 (Monitoring understanding). This code suggests: making requests (Speak slowly, Can I go..., please?) responding to requests (Yes. Ok. No, sorry.), suggesting something (Can you..?/Let's play), offering help (Can I help you?), monitoring understanding (Does he understand?/Can you spell your name?/How do you say it in English?/Can you repeat it please?). Code 10 "suasion - advising, persuading, urging" develops pragmatic competences and this code appears to be sufficiently represented for the A1 level of language proficiency.

The following codes were mentioned three times, twice or once. Code number 11 "socialising" was mentioned in the introduction of the curriculum and in competences 18 (Correspondence) and 19 (Making a phone call). This code includes: written greetings, letters (how to start and finish) and telephone conversations. It is believed that this code was sufficient enough for this language proficiency in the development of pragmatic competences. Code number 5 "appropriate use of please and thank you" was illustrated in competences 1 (Relating with others in a communicative situation), 14 (Making and responding to offers) with phrases such as: thank you; thanks; that's ok; OK; yes, please; no, thank you. There were good examples for thanking in the described situations, but an explanation for the different variations of using "please" was missing. Code numbers 3 "positive politeness" and 6 "impoliteness" were mentioned only once in competence 9 (Discussing interests and tastes). These codes were not sufficient with only very simple phrases expressing likes and dislikes (I like/I love, I don't like). All the mentioned codes (3, 6, 9) develop the sociolinguistic and pragmatic competences.

Code number 21 "ritual behaviour" was mentioned only once in the topics for communication "Multicultural society" with the suggestions for discussions: foreign languages, celebrations, cultures coming together. This belongs to the category of socio-cultural knowledge and the elaboration of this category in the national curriculum was inadequate.

The category of recommended materials was never mentioned in the curriculum and the category of recommended methods and techniques was mentioned only once in code 28 "creating portfolio". The part dealing with evaluation and the portfolio included self-evaluating notes, collection of drawings, projects, tests, etc.

To summarize, some of the codes were well described and represented, some were sufficient, some were insufficient and quite a significant number of codes were not even mentioned in the current national curriculum. For example, code number 1 "greetings, addressing" and code number 10 "suasion - advising, persuading, urging" were well represented with lots of appropriate examples with the aim to develop the sociolinguistic and pragmatic competences. Codes 11 "socialising" and 5 "appropriate use of please and thank you" are considered as fairly sufficient (telephone conversations, written greetings, thanking), but there were some essential parts of these codes missing (how to use 'please' appropriately, socializing – greetings, conversations). These codes develop sociolinguistic and pragmatic competences. Code numbers 3 "positive politeness" and 6 "Impoliteness" are believed as insufficient, as they only mentioned very simple phrases (I like/I don't like) for expressing likes and dislikes. Socio-cultural knowledge was represented only by code 21 "ritual behaviour" with only basic topics mentioned (foreign languages, celebrations, cultures coming together). This category was insufficiently represented in the current curriculum. 19 out of 29 codes were not even mentioned in the curriculum and it is believed that code numbers 2 "use of exclamations", and 4 "negative politeness", and at least some codes connected with the categories of non-verbal communication, materials, techniques and methods for teaching culture should be included in the national curriculum.

4.1.4. Conclusion of the document analyses

The aim of the document analyses was to analyse the cultural aspects in the Slovak curricular documents (pre-reform and current) for teaching English at a primary school level and to compare them to the cultural aspects in the CEFR. Another aim was to compare the two Slovak curricular documents, the pre-reform curriculum (2001) and the current national curriculum (2011). 6 categories and 29 codes concerning cultural aspects were developed and these were based on the CEFR. Based on these 29 codes, I have analysed both Slovak curricular documents and discussed the strengths and faults of both documents above. The other aim was to see if there was a positive shift in the current curriculum regarding cultural contents with reference to the CERF. The findings of this analysis are in the following table:

Categories	Codes	Pre-reform curriculum (2001)	Current national curriculum (2011)
Sociolinguistic competences	1 greetings, addressing	5 times - insufficient	4 times – very good
	2 use of exclamations	0	0
	3 positive politeness	5 times - sufficient	1 time - insufficient
	4 negative politeness	2 times - insufficient	0
	5 appropriate use of	1 time - insufficient	2 times - sufficient
	6 impoliteness	1 time - sufficient	1 time – insufficient
	7 proverbs, idioms	0	0
	8 register (language use in different contexts) (p. 120)	0	0
	9 dialect, accent (p. 121)	0	0
Pragmatic competences	10 suasion (advising, persuading, urging) (p. 126)	0	4 times – very good
	11 socialising (p. 126)	2 times - sufficient	3 times – sufficient
	12 interaction patterns (127)	0	0
Non-verbal communication	13 body language (p. 89)	0	0
	14 extra linguistic speech sounds (p. 89)	0	0
	15 prosodic qualities (p. 89)	0	0

Categories	Codes	Pre-reform curriculum (2001)	Current national curriculum (2011)
Socio-cultural knowledge	16 everyday living (p. 102)	3 times - sufficient	0
	17 living conditions (p. 102)	0	0
	18 interpersonal relations (p. 102)	1 time - sufficient	0
	19 values, beliefs, attitudes, people, country (p. 103)	5 times – very good	0
	20 social conventions (p. 103)	0	0
	21 ritual behaviour (p. 103)	5 times – very good	0
Recommended materials	22 authentic texts	0	0
	23 authentic language (p. 56, 143, 148, 154)	0	0
	24 special books (p. 148)	0	0
	25 computers (p. 143)	0	0
Recommended methods and techniques	26 role-plays, games, simulations (p. 56, 148)	0	0
	27 discussions, negotiations (p. 145, 148)	0	0
	28 explanations, illustrations (p. 145, 148)	0	0
	29 creating portfolios (p. 175)	0	1 time - sufficient

Table 5: Comparison of the pre reform curriculum and the current curriculum

I have decided to mark the quality of the included codes as "very good", "sufficient", and "insufficient", based on the above analyses of the contents of the mentioned codes. It is evident (Table 6), that there is a noticeable difference between what aspects of culture were included in the pre-reform curriculum and the current national curriculum. Each curriculum had some very well documented codes, some codes were sufficient, some codes were insufficient and quite a number of codes were not included at all.

The pre-reform curriculum included five codes and the current curriculum included four codes out of nine from the sociolinguistic competences category. Out of the five codes in the pre-reform curriculum only two codes (3, 6) were sufficient and three codes (1, 4, 5) were insufficient. Out of the four codes in the current curriculum one code (1) was very good, one code (5) was sufficient and two codes (3, 6) were insufficient. Overall, the category of sociolinguistic competences was equally represented in both curricular documents, with a similar number of codes and level of quality. However, what was good in the pre-reform document was worsened in the current document, and vice versa. Both curricula were still missing four or five other codes from this category, from which the codes describing negative politeness, or exclamations should be included.

Out of three codes the category of pragmatic competences was only represented by one code (11) in the pre-reform curriculum and by two codes (10, 11) in the current curriculum. Code 11 in the pre-reform curriculum is considered as sufficient. The current curriculum was represented by two codes, from which one code (10) was very good and the second one (11) was sufficient. Overall, the category of pragmatic competences was significantly better represented by the current curriculum, from which two codes were either very well or sufficiently represented. The pre-reform curriculum mentioned one code, which was sufficient, but two codes were missing.

The category of socio-cultural knowledge was represented by 4 codes out of 6 (16, 18, 19, 21) in the pre-reform curriculum and by one code (21) in the current curriculum. In the pre-reform curriculum, two codes (19, 21) were very good, and two codes (16, 18) were sufficient, but there were still two codes missing. The current curriculum mentioned only one code (21) out of six and it is believed that this code is insufficient as it is too general with little information. Overall, the category of socio-cultural knowledge was significantly better represented by the pre-reform curriculum, which included two very good codes and two sufficient codes. The current curriculum was poor in terms of including socio-cultural knowledge into its content, as it lacked basic information.

From the category of recommended methods and techniques, the current curriculum only included one code (28) and it is believed to be sufficient. Nevertheless, out of four codes in this category, only one was mentioned. The pre-reform curriculum did not mention any codes. This category was under-represented in both curricular documents.

Neither curricular documents included the categories of non-verbal communication and recommended materials. These categories should be included, because non-verbal communication is an important part of intercultural communication and the category of recommended materials offers valuable tips for materials which could be used for cultural teaching.

There is one important thing to mention, that there is not always a parallel with the number of occurrences and the quality of the codes. For example, in the pre-reform curriculum, code number 1 "greetings, addressing" was present five times and considering the contents it is believed to be insufficient. On the other hand, code number 6 "impoliteness" was present only once and I consider it as sufficient, because it was very well described with adequate examples. Similar inadequacies can be found in more cases in both curricular documents. However on the other hand, the codes which are considered as very good also have high occurrences in the curricular documents (four or five times).

To summarize both curricular documents, the research questions have to be answered. **Research question number 1** (from the research questions with regard to the main aim) states:

1. **How are the recommended cultural contents from CEFR reflected in the current Slovak curriculum?**

- Only 8 codes out of 29 were included in the current curriculum, from which not all the codes were equally well represented.
- The sociolinguistic competence category was represented by 4 out of 9 codes, the pragmatic competence category was represented by 2 out of 3 codes and the socio-cultural knowledge category was represented only by 1 out of 6 codes. All the categories in the current Slovak curriculum should be amended, because even most of the included codes did not sufficiently reflect the CEFR.
- The category of recommended methods and techniques was only represented by 1 out of 4 codes.
- Other categories including non-verbal communication and recommended materials were not mentioned.

Research question number 1 (from the further research questions) states:

1. **To what extent do the Slovak curricular documents reflect the CEFR concerning the implementation of cultural teaching within the English**

language education and is there a positive shift in the current curriculum in comparison with the pre-reform curriculum?

- The extent of cultural teaching in both curricula is considered as generally insufficient.
- The current curriculum only included 8 out of 29 codes and the pre-reform curriculum included 10 out of 29 codes. Not all the codes have the equal importance, but it is believed that some important categories and codes, e.g. negative politeness, exclamations, living conditions, social conventions, non-verbal communication, recommended materials, methods and techniques should be included.
- The study cannot say with certainty whether the shift was generally positive or negative, as some cultural aspects were represented better than others and some were not even mentioned. A positive shift can be seen in the development of competences, but a negative shift can be seen in the area of socio-cultural knowledge. Considering the number of codes or indeed the lack in the number of codes present, the cultural aspects of language teaching in both curricular documents are deemed to be insufficient and somewhat wanting.

4.2. Observation analyses

The method of observation was chosen as the primary method of research for this project as it allowed for the collection of the most authentic and reliable data. The aim of carrying out the observations was to capture a picture of the real situation in English language lessons taught at primary schools in Slovakia, and more specifically to identify, analyse and explain what and how cultural aspects are taught.

The 'observer-as-participant' form of observation was carried out, where the researcher was known to the group, but did not have much contact with them. The observer-as-participant observation was carried out in 50 English lessons. These lessons were conducted by 30 English language teachers in different schools in the Nitra region. All the teachers were informed about the aim of the research and were asked to include some cultural teaching in their lessons (what they normally do). The amount and content were left up to them to decide. The researcher sat in the back of each class, where she took notes in accordance with the observation scheme, which included five main categories (see Table 7 below) and was prepared beforehand. Some of the categories were modified as the research progressed. Also the technique of taking field notes was applied to capture the progress and what was happening in the lessons. It was initially planned to record the observed lessons, but the teachers did not give their consent.

The observation scheme was used to assess the cultural teaching during all the observed lessons. The entries in the scheme included: aim, extent, integration and contents of cultural teaching; competences, skills and critical thinking developed by cultural teaching; materials, methods used for cultural teaching, and any problems which arose during the lessons.

For the analyses, a system of categories and codes was created based on the observation schedule and the field notes. Five main categories were created, which included several particular codes. For clarification, the categories and codes are summarised in the following table:

Category: 1. Presence of cultural teaching
Codes:
1. YES 2. NO 3. Culture integrated within the topic 4. Culture taught separately 5. Pupils' involvement in cultural teaching
Category: 2. Contents of cultural teaching
Codes:
1. Visible culture 2. Invisible culture 3. Socio-cultural knowledge 4. Sociolinguistic competence 5. Pragmatic competence 6. Paralinguistic competence
Category: 3. Materials used for cultural teaching
Codes:
1. School books 2. Non authentic materials 3. Authentic materials
Category: 4. Methods and techniques used for cultural teaching
Codes:
1. Explanation by a teacher 2. Role play 3. Games 4. Field trip 5. Discussions, comparisons 6. Drama 7. Cultural island 8. Noticing 9. Reformulation

10. Predicting	
11. Treasure hunt	
12. Singing	
13. Projects	
14. Others	
Category: 5. Skills and linguistic aspects developed by cultural teaching	
Codes:	
1. Reading	
2. Listening	
3. Writing	
4. Speaking	
5. Grammar	
6. Vocabulary	
7. Pronunciation	

Table 7: Categories and codes for observation analyses

This system of categories and codes was applied to all 50 observed lessons. As the categories and codes are so extensive, for better understanding and clarity, each category is analysed individually.

The first category "Presence of cultural teaching" presents information concerning whether the observed teachers included cultural aspects in their lessons and if the cultural aspects were integrated within the topic and if the pupils were involved in the cultural teaching. It has to be borne in mind that all the observed teachers were informed about the aim of the research and were asked to include some cultural teaching in their lessons.

Code numbers 1 and 2 deal with the presence of cultural teaching in the observed lessons. In spite of the knowledge about the aim of the research, only 24 out of 50 lessons included some cultural aspects. The finding that only just under half of the lessons included cultural aspects is alarming, especially considering the fact that all the teachers were asked to involve some cultural teaching in their lessons.

All the following analyses are based on the 24 lessons, which included cultural aspects. 12 out of the 24 lessons dedicated between 15 to 35 minutes to cultural teaching. This indicates that cultural teaching was an essential part of the observed lessons, but it was usually combined with some other topics, or grammar. It needs to be mentioned, that the amount of time spent on cultural teaching was not as an important consideration as the contents and integration of cultural aspects in the language lessons. Some of the lessons were chopped up into separate, independent parts and appeared confusing. However, some lessons integrated cultural issues into the main topic. However other lessons failed to integrate the cultural aspects into the language teaching; for example, in one lesson, a teacher revised facts about the USA – a topic from a book – and then carried on with new grammar on comparatives, without any connection to the previous topic. The lesson appeared to be artificially divided up into two separate parts. A similar example of separating a lesson into three different parts was done by a teacher, who spent a part of the lesson revising vocabulary on insects, a part on doing simple arithmetic exercises in English and a part on Easter traditions in England. On the other hand, a very good example of the integration of cultural teaching was a lesson on shopping and a teacher included a shopping role-play using authentic materials for about 25 minutes, where the pupils were using sociolinguistic and pragmatic phrases needed for shopping. Surprisingly, this teacher was not even aware of developing intercultural communicative competences with her pupils and of the importance of using authentic materials. Another example illustrates how well cultural issues can be implemented into teaching grammatical structures. The aim of the lesson was to teach comparatives and superlatives. The teacher used geographical places (rivers, towns, countries) for creating sentences using comparatives and superlatives.

8 lessons out of 24 dedicated between 35–45 minutes to cultural teaching. From these 8 lessons, in most cases (5) the teachers spent the whole lesson doing "cultural pages" from their text books. Nowadays, many books include so called "cultural pages". Unfortunately, the observed teachers just went through the cultural pages superficially by reading the texts, translating them into Slovak and doing comprehensive exercises. Any deeper explanation, discussion, understanding, awareness and questions were missing. On the other hand, there was a teacher who dedicated the whole lesson to the presentation of pupils' projects on famous British people. The pupils prepared power point presentations, with the length and contents suitable for their age. Another case illustrates how some great ideas can be used badly. This particular teacher dedicated the whole lesson to cultural teaching. She had great ideas, used authentic materials (magazines, a fish and chip's box, an English film), but the lessons were totally confusing. The teacher almost always spoke in Slovak, tried to cover too many issues, jumped from one thing to another, asked questions and then answered them herself. The material being taught was also well above the pupils' abilities; the pupils seemed to be confused and struggled with the basic vocabulary and pronunciation.

Only 4 lessons included between 5 to 15 minutes of cultural teaching. This means that the teachers used some cultural aspects as complementary teaching to their topics. For example, one topic was about describing people and the teacher prepared a poster with pictures of famous British and American people. Pupils were to guess who they were, and which country they were from. In this case, cultural aspects were cleverly integrated into the main topic of the lesson.

Code numbers 3 and 4 refer to the integration of cultural teaching within the main topic of the lessons or teaching cultural aspects in a separate topic. Overall 18 lessons integrated cultural aspects with the main topics of the lessons. 8 out of 24 lessons either dedicated the whole lessons to cultural teaching or integrated it into the lesson topic. From what has been discussed above, it is evident that even if the whole lesson is dedicated to cultural issues, it does not always lead to efficient cultural learning (instead at times it can lead to superficial teaching, confusing lessons, and difficult materials).

From the 12 lessons (where between 15 to 35 minutes was dedicated to cultural teaching), only 6 lessons integrated cultural teaching into the main topic of the lesson. The other 6 lessons were made up from two or more separate parts, where cultural teaching was one of them and it had no connection with the other part (examples were discussed earlier).

All 4 lessons, which dedicated 5 to 15 minutes of cultural teaching, included cultural aspects in the main topic of the lesson. Perhaps the most efficient way to develop intercultural communicative competences was achieved by a teacher, who was using pragmatic and sociolinguistic phrases such as: "bless you", "enjoy your meal", "learn it off by heart", "cheers", etc. The teacher and pupils used such phrases naturally during the lesson, whenever it was needed. It is important to mention the fact, that this teacher was unaware that she was including cultural issues into her teaching. It is assumed that the reason why she was doing it naturally is because she was married to an Englishman and from her personal experience she knew how important it is to know pragmatic and sociolinguistic phrases.

Code number 5 refers to the pupils' involvement in lessons. This means whether only the teachers talked, or pupils were involved in the lessons by discussing, comparing, and doing various activities during cultural teaching. In 17 out of 24 lessons, pupils were involved in cultural teaching (role-play, shopping, comparisons of Slovak and English Easter traditions, Easter egg hunt game, discussions on sightseeing in Nitra and finding countries and towns on a map, presenting projects, completing exercises in books). In the remaining 6 lessons, cultural aspects were only introduced by the teachers, with no further references or discussions.

The above examples prove that the amount of time is not the main indicator of the quality of cultural teaching. In some cases, when a greater part of the lesson was dedicated to cultural teaching the result was very poor often with confused pupils. On the other hand, some lessons managed to deliver better results with brief, but integrated issues within the main topic of the lesson.

For a better illustration the above information is described in the following table:

Category: 1. Presence of cultural teaching		
1. YES	24 lessons (out of 50) 48%	8 lessons (35 – 45 min.)
		12 lessons (15 – 35 min.)
		4 lessons (5 – 15 min.)
2. NO	26 lessons (out of 50) = 52%	
3. Culture integrated within the topic	lessons (out of 24) = 75%	
4. Culture taught separately	6 lessons (out of 24) = 25%	
5. Pupils' involvement in cultural teaching	YES 17 lessons (out of 24) 71%	NO 6 lessons (out of 24) 29%

Table 8:   Presence of cultural teaching

The second category "Contents of cultural teaching" deals with the subjects of cultural teaching, whether it was focused more on visible or invisible parts (based on the iceberg concept of culture), what socio-cultural knowledge was included, and which competences were developed (sociolinguistic, pragmatic, paralinguistic).

Code numbers 1 and 2 in this second category focused on the two levels of culture. Brembec's iceberg concept of culture (in Levine and Adelman, 1993; Afs Intl, 1984) was chosen for the analysis, where the visible part includes countries, towns, fine arts, literature, music, folklore, theatre, architecture, food, clothes, holidays, etc., and the invisible part includes conversational patterns, language, dialects, accents, interaction between sexes, generations, social groups, perception of the self and others, body language, gestures, mimics, proxemics, eye contact, voice loudness, etc.

From the 24 observed lessons, which included cultural teaching, 21 lessons focused on the "visible" part of culture. 10 lessons concentrated on people, places and countries, 3 lessons on housing, 2 lessons on food, 2 on schools, 2 on Easter and 2 on heroes. Only 4 lessons out of 24 dealt with the "invisible" part of the culture, which included the use of language (phrases) useful for intercultural communication. 1 lesson combined both, the visible and invisible parts of culture. Unfortunately this lesson was conducted by the teacher (mentioned above), who had great ideas, but was unable to fulfil their implementation properly and in a satisfactory manner. She spoke most of the time, did not involve pupils enough in her lessons and she spoke mainly in Slovak. She described a typical Christmas meal to her pupils, talked about "curry" becoming the most popular food in the UK, described "chips" being an American name and "French fries" being an English name (which is also wrong), and told students to use the correct phrase "Enjoy your meal" before eating. The intention was good, but the outcome was unsatisfactory for an English lesson, where pupils should be exposed to the English language, practice their English and develop competences and not only listen to their teacher.

Code number 3 "socio-cultural knowledge" is closely connected with the visible part of culture. 21 lessons out of 24 included socio-cultural knowledge. This means that the teachers concentrated mainly on acquiring knowledge about aspects of the foreign culture. 10 lessons focused on people, places and countries, such as facts about the UK, USA, Australia, London, Nitra, people of different nationalities living in the UK. 3 lessons focused on housing, where the teacher described and showed pupils types of houses in the UK. 2 lessons dealt with knowledge about English food, such as the traditional Christmas meal, Yorkshire pudding, roast beef, curry, and a full English breakfast. 2 lessons briefly dealt with information about English schools, just mentioning uniforms and school plays. 2 lessons referred to Easter traditions in the UK and 2 lessons dealt with heroes, celebrities or other famous people from the UK or the USA. In another lesson pupils presented their own power point projects about famous people (e.g. David Beckham, William Shakespeare, Queen Elizabeth II.). This proved to be a very efficient and effective method of student empowerment and encouraging students to practice their English and develop intercultural competences.

Code numbers 4, 5 and 6 are closely connected with the invisible part of culture. Code number 4 "Sociolinguistic competence" refers to the socio-cultural conditions of language use. Acquiring sociolinguistic competences relates to the ability to use the correct language, phrases, words for greetings, addressing people, exclamations, positive and negative politeness, impoliteness, etc. Also the correct use of please and thank you, proverbs, idioms, dialects and accents belongs to the sociolinguistic competence. Code number 5 "Pragmatic competence" is concerned with the functional use of language, where the cultural component is as important as the ability to use the language suitably for the particular culture. The pragmatic competence includes the ability to advise, persuade, request, offer, socialize, suggest, take turns in conversation, etc. The code 6 "Paralinguistic competence" refers to the non-verbal communication, body language, extralinguistic speech sounds and prosodic qualities of the voice. These are all important features in intercultural communication, which can cause misunderstandings when perceived or performed inappropriately. The three competences are closely connected and interlinked and cannot be used separately in communication.

It was mentioned earlier, that only 4 lessons dealt with the invisible part of culture. 3 lessons included sociolinguistic phrases and all 4 lessons included pragmatic phrases and none of the observed lessons included aspects of paralinguistic competences. The sociolinguistic competences were developed through practicing greetings, politeness, impoliteness, idioms and use of 'please' and 'thank you' (Yes, please.; No, thank you.; Good afternoon.; Hello.; Good bye.; Bless you.; Cheers.; Learn it off by heart.; Leave me alone.). The pragmatic competences were developed through practicing offers, requests, suggestions (Can I have…; How can I help you?; Would you like something else?; Enjoy your meal.; Here you are.; Can I borrow a tissue please?). In 3 lessons out of 4, the phrases were used actively by the pupils either in a role play, or during the lesson whenever a certain phrase was suitable to use. The fact that only 4 out of 50 observed lessons paid attention to the invisible part of culture. This is very disappointing considering that the invisible part of culture is, in reality, the main component of developing ICC. Paralinguistic competences were never included, even though their importance in intercultural communication is immense, as more than 2/3 of communication is non-verbal.

For a better illustration, the figures are summarized in the following table:

Category: 2. Contents of cultural teaching	Occurrence
Codes:	
1. Visible culture	21 lessons (out of 24) = 85%
2. Invisible culture	4 lessons (out of 24) = 17%
3. Socio-cultural knowledge	21 lessons (out of 24) = 85%
4. Sociolinguistic competence	3 lessons (out of 24) = 13%
5. Pragmatic competence	4 lessons (out of 24) = 17%
6. Paralinguistic competence	0 lessons (out of 24) = 0%

Table 9:   Contents of cultural teaching

The third category "Materials used for cultural teaching" focuses on the types of materials the teachers used during their observed lessons. In 13 lessons school books were used, in 9 lessons non-authentic materials were used and in 9 lessons authentic materials were used. In 8 lessons a combination of different materials was used. The non-authentic materials included flash cards, "Hello" magazine (a Slovak magazine written in English for Slovak pupils), educational DVDs, school maps, student-made posters, power point presentations. The authentic materials included John Lennon's song "Imagine" from youtube, photos of famous people, Mr Noisy, Mr Happy & Mr Lazy books (English children books), Easter eggs, a Romeo & Juliet DVD, a Fish & Chips box, toys of shopping products (which were original English toys and virtually identical copies of real things), the teachers' own pictures of Bournemouth. Authentic materials are considered as attractive and efficient resources for teaching culture in foreign language classrooms, because they bring reality to the classroom and the learners can come into contact with the real-life language, which can be a great motivational factor. It is deemed to be completely insufficient that only 9 out of the 50 observed lessons used some authentic materials (to a certain extent).

For a better illustration, the figures are summarised in the following table:

Category: 3. Materials used for cultural teaching	Occurrence
Codes:	
1. School books	13 lessons (out of 24) = 54%
2. Non authentic materials	9 lessons (out of 24) = 38%
3. Authentic materials	9 lessons (out of 24) = 38%

Table 10: Materials used for cultural teaching

The fourth category "Methods and techniques used for cultural teaching" analyses the methods and techniques that were used during the English lessons. A list of 14 methods and techniques were created for this research, which was based on the recommendations of the CEFR (2001), Cullen (2000), and Hughes (1986) for cultural teaching. Most of the observed lessons (19) used only one method or technique for cultural teaching. 5 lessons used a combination of methods and techniques (e.g. discussion, comparison, noticing and singing). However, one lesson combined a game, discussion, singing and a homework assignment of a project.

The most common methods were discussions and comparisons (code 5) of cultural features, which was used in 9 lessons. For example Robin Hood was discussed and compared to the Slovak folk hero Jánošík; English and American towns and cities (London, Washington, Bristol) were discussed and compared with Bratislava and Nitra; the advantages and disadvantages of English school uniforms were discussed; Easter traditions in Slovakia and the UK were compared; and immigrants in the UK and Slovakia were also briefly discussed.

The method of explanation by a teacher (code 1) was used in 7 lessons. For example, the teachers explained the Easter traditions in the UK, meals and meal times in the UK, the tradition of school plays, etc. Further discussions or comparisons would have been more beneficial for the cultural awareness of pupils, but were not present after the teachers' explanations.

6 English classes took place in dedicated language classrooms, where posters, pictures, maps and objects were on the walls or shelves. These classrooms were to create a "cultural island" (code 7), where pupils could experience the atmosphere of the English language and culture. Regretfully, the posters and pictures were not always contemporary and attractive, which would have met the goals of an effective cultural island. Instead, uninspiring posters advertising language books, dictionaries, or grammar charts were often used. However it must also be noted that attractive posters of contemporary teenage stars, pictures of the English countryside, maps and authentic objects were found in some classrooms.

The elaboration of school book exercises (code 14 others) was present in 5 lessons, where pupils completed exercises in the cultural pages in their school books.

4 lessons used the method of projects (code 13) as a part of cultural teaching. In 3 cases, projects were to be done as homework. The pupils were to prepare food recipes, posters of personal heroes, drawings and descriptions of foreigners in Slovakia. One observed lesson was dedicated to the presentation of pupils' projects on British heroes and famous people (W. Shakespeare, D. Beckham, Queen Elizabeth II., A. Christie, J. Lennon, W. Churchill).

Singing a song (code 12) with cultural context was used during 3 lessons. One song was about a town, another was an Easter song and the last one was "Imagine" by John Lennon. In all 3 cases singing a song was a complementary activity to the main cultural topic.

A role play (code 2) was used during 2 lessons. Both lessons used a role play on practicing shopping activities, using pragmatic and sociolinguistic phrases necessary for effective intercultural communication. One of them was particularly attractive for the pupils, as it used authentic materials (a shopping role play).

Games (code 3) were used during 2 lessons. Both lessons used an "Egg hunting" game, where plastic or chocolate Easter eggs were hidden in the classroom and pupils were looking for them. One lesson combined an "Egg hunting" game with doing a kind of handicrafts task, which comprised of drawing, colouring, and cutting out from paper a basket with little eggs, and gluing them together to create an Easter basket.

Noticing (code 8) was used during 2 lessons. In both cases, the topics of the lessons were towns and places and the teachers brought maps and pupils had to find the discussed towns, cities, countries on the map (UK, USA, London, Washington, etc.)

Using sociolinguistic and pragmatic phrases (where suitable) was present in one lesson (code 14 others). The teacher used phrases and taught pupils to use phrases such as "Yes, please.; No, thank you.; Bless you.; Cheers.; Learn it off by heart.; Leave me alone; Here you are.; Can I borrow a tissue please?..." as they would use in their everyday life.

For a better illustration, the findings are summarised in the following table:

Category: 4. Methods and techniques used for cultural teaching	Occurrence
Codes:	
1. Explanation by a teacher	7 lessons (out of 24) = 29%
2. Role play	2 lessons (out of 24) = 8%
3. Games	2 lessons (out of 24) = 8%
4. Field trip	0 lessons (out of 24) = 0%
5. Discussions, comparisons	9 lessons (out of 24) = 38%
6. Drama	0 lessons (out of 24) = 0%
7. Cultural island	6 lessons (out of 24) = 25%
8. Noticing	2 lessons (out of 24) = 8%
9. Reformulation	0 lessons (out of 24) = 0%
10. Predicting	0 lessons (out of 24) = 0%
11. Treasure hunt	0 lessons (out of 24) = 0%
12. Singing	3 lessons (out of 24) = 13%
13. Projects	4 lessons (out of 24) = 17%
14. Others (school book exercises, real life practicing)	7 lessons (out of 24) = 29%

Table 11: Methods and techniques used for cultural teaching

It is a generally accepted fact nowadays, that cultural considerations are intrinsic to language instruction. Culture should be an integral part of all language skills (reading, listening, speaking and writing) and should not be treated as an extra skill.

The fifth category analyses "Skills and linguistic aspects developed by cultural teaching". This category includes developing all language skills and acquiring cultural vocabulary, correct pronunciation of culturally specific words and also learning grammatical structures through cultural teaching. It is very difficult to decide and single out, which skills or linguistic aspects were developed through cultural teaching, because certain skills and linguistic aspects are a part of every language lesson and can be interlinked with cultural teaching (which is the ideal). "Cultural pages" in the school books are designed to cover most or all language skills. There is normally a text to read and a listening to listen to, plus comprehension exercises for writing and suggestions for speaking activities. However, mainly reading and listening activities prevailed in the materials used in the observed lessons.

The most frequent skill developed in the cultural teaching was "speaking" (code 4), which was present in 11 out of 24 lessons. Even though speaking skills had the highest occurrence (11), it was present in only less than half of the lessons (24), where culture was taught. The speaking activities varied from effective role plays (2), project presentations (1), using phrases in real life situations (1), descriptions of people and places (4), to less effective techniques such as answering comprehension questions (3). The lessons with role plays and project presentations were the most effective ways in developing speaking skills.

"Reading" skills (code 1) were developed in 10 out of 24 lessons. Most texts (8) for cultural teaching were taken from the school books' "cultural pages" (places, people). Sadly the activity usually boiled down to pupils just reading the texts, translating them and answering comprehension questions. Sometimes (3) the reading activity was combined with some discussion or descriptions of the people and places. In two cases, English magazines for Slovak school children (Hello) were used, with articles on heroes and Australia. In the case of all the reading activities, translation from English to Slovak was applied, which was not always necessary.

"Listening" skills (code 2) were developed in 8 out of 24 lessons. In three cases the CD recordings (about schools, food and towns) were combined with the school texts, in three cases video recordings (about towns,, Great Britain and a Romeo and Juliet film) were used and in two cases Easter songs were used. The video recordings were attractive tools for the pupils, but the teachers only played them, occasionally stopped them and explained, or translated the contexts of the recordings to pupils. There were no interesting activities to go with the recordings, which was a missed opportunity to use videos for educational purposes rather than just a time for pupils to passively watch something they did not always understand.

"Writing" skills (code 3) were developed in 6 out of 24 lessons. Three writing activities were limited only to completing comprehensive exercises, twice the writing activity was based on writing sentences describing people, and one activity was on writing new vocabulary. Completing exercises was the most-used writing activity and it is believed to be the least effective in developing writing skills.

Nine lessons involved new cultural vocabulary (code 6) on food (baked beans, Yorkshire pudding, curry), houses (detached, semi-detached, terraced, flat, bungalow), pragmatic and sociolinguistic phrases (Bless you, Here you are), shops, places, school subjects, Easter vocabulary, etc.

94

In two cases grammatical structures (code 5) were practiced with cultural contents. In both lessons, comparatives and superlatives were practiced with the knowledge of geographical places (rivers, towns, countries). This was an effective way to use geographical places for learning and practicing grammar, where cultural knowledge is also practiced.

Two lessons dealt with learning the correct pronunciation of places, towns and countries. One teacher even phonemically transcribed the proper names (e.g. Manchester, Birmingham, Chinese) on the board, pupils had no problems with the phonemic symbols and could read and pronounce the words well. Another teacher used a CD recording for the correct pronunciation of names of places (e.g. the Nile, Egypt, Europe). The names of countries are often problematic for pronunciation, as the names are similar in many languages and people tend to pronounce them the same way as they do in their own languages, which can cause misunderstandings. Unfortunately, only two teachers paid special attention to the correct pronunciation.

For a better illustration, the findings are summarised in the following table:

Category: 5. Skills and linguistic aspects developed by cultural teaching	Occurrence	
Codes:		Types of activities
1. Reading	10 lessons (out of 24) 42%	8 texts from 'cultural pages' 2 texts from the 'Hello' magazine
2. Listening	8 lessons (out of 24) 33%	6 CD recordings 2 DVDs
3. Writing	6 lessons (out of 24) 25%	3 completing exercises 2 writing sentences 1 writing vocabulary
4. Speaking	11 lessons (out of 24) 46%	4 description of people and places 3 answering questions 2 role plays 1 project presentation 1 real life situations
5. Grammar	2 lessons (out of 24) 8%	2 comparatives and superlatives

Category: 5. Skills and linguistic aspects developed by cultural teaching	Occurrence	
6. Vocabulary	6 lessons (out of 24) 25%	Food, houses, shops, places, phrases, school subjects, Easter vocabulary
7. Pronunciation	2 lessons (out of 24) 8%	Proper names (the Nile, Egypt, Europe, Manchester, Birmingham, Chinese)

Table 12:   Skills and linguistic aspects developed by cultural teaching

4.2.1. Conclusion of the observation analyses

The aim of the observation analyses was to provide an outline of the real situation of cultural teaching in English language lessons (50) at primary schools in the Nitra region. 5 main categories, each including several codes, were created for the analyses. We analysed each category individually above.

For a better illustration, a summary of all the categories and codes can be found in the following table:

Category: 1. Presence of cultural teaching	
Codes:	
1. YES	24 lessons (out of 50) = 48%
2. NO	26 lessons (out of 50) = 52%
3. Culture integrated within the topic	18 lessons (out of 24) = 75%
4. Culture taught separately	6 lessons (out of 24) = 25%
5. Pupils' involvement in cultural teaching	YES 17 lessons (out of 24) = 71% NO 7 lessons (out of 24) = 29%
Category: 2. Contents of cultural teaching	
Codes:	
1. Visible culture	21 lessons (out of 24) = 85%
2. Invisible culture	4 lessons (out of 24) = 17%
3. Socio-cultural knowledge	21 lessons (out of 24) = 85%
4. Sociolinguistic competence	3 lessons (out of 24) = 13%
5. Pragmatic competence	4 lessons (out of 24) = 17%
6. Paralinguistic competence	0 lessons (out of 24) = 0%

Category: 3. Materials used for cultural teaching	
Codes:	
1. School books	13 lessons (out of 24) = 54%
2. Non authentic materials	9 lessons (out of 24) = 38%
3. Authentic materials	9 lessons (out of 24) = 38%
Category: 4. Methods and techniques used for cultural teaching	
Codes:	
1. Explanation by a teacher	7 lessons (out of 24) = 29%
2. Role play	2 lessons (out of 24) = 8%
3. Games	2 lessons (out of 24) = 8%
4. Field trip	0 lessons (out of 24) = 0%
5. Discussions, comparisons	9 lessons (out of 24) = 38%
6. Drama	0 lessons (out of 24) = 0%
7. Cultural island	6 lessons (out of 24) = 25%
8. Noticing	2 lessons (out of 24) = 8%
9. Reformulation	0 lessons (out of 24) = 0%
10. Predicting	0 lessons (out of 24) = 0%
11. Treasure hunt	0 lessons (out of 24) = 0%
12. Singing	3 lessons (out of 24) = 13%
13. Projects	4 lessons (out of 24) = 17%
14. Others	7 lessons (out of 24) = 29%
Category: 5. Skills and linguistic aspects developed by cultural teaching	
Codes:	
1. Reading	10 lessons (out of 24) = 42%
2. Listening	8 lessons (out of 24) = 33%
3. Writing	6 lessons (out of 24) = 25%
4. Speaking	11 lessons (out of 24) = 46%
5. Grammar	2 lessons (out of 24) = 8%
6. Vocabulary	6 lessons (out of 24) = 25%
7. Pronunciation	2 lessons (out of 24) = 8%

Table 13: Summary of observation analyses

To summarize the observation analyses, research questions need to be answered. **Research question number 2** (from the research questions with regard to the main aim) states:

"Which techniques are used for cultural teaching in English lessons in primary education in Slovakia?"

- The following techniques were used for cultural teaching in the observed lessons: discussions and comparisons (9), explanations by a teacher (7), cultural islands (6), projects (4), noticing (2), games (2) and role plays (2).
- Most of the lessons (19) included 1 technique and 5 lessons used a combination of two or more techniques.
- Most of the lessons included uninteresting and ineffective techniques, which did not capture the attention or motivate the pupils not only for cultural learning but also for foreign language learning.

Research question number 3 (from the research questions with regard to the main aim) states:
"What materials are used for cultural teaching in English lessons in primary education in Slovakia?"

- The most used material for cultural teaching was a school book (13).
- Non-authentic materials (the Slovak magazine "Hello" written in English for Slovak pupils, school maps, self created posters, power point presentations, educational DVDs were used in 9 lessons.
- Authentic materials were used in 9 lessons. These included a song, Easter eggs, a DVD, children books, toys representing actual branded products (cans of backed beans, milk bottles, packets of biscuits, boxes of cereals, fresh fruit and vegetables), a fish n' chips box and a teachers' own photographs.
- 8 lessons included a combination of different materials.

From the observed lessons, it can be concluded, that the lessons which included the combination of various materials and methods for cultural teaching were the most effective and motivating visibly capturing the attention of the pupils. However, out of the 24 lessons which included cultural teaching, sadly only a few lessons fulfilled the criteria for an interesting and effective lesson in developing intercultural communicative competences.

4.3. Interview analyses

The third method chosen for the current research was to conduct interviews with the English teachers. With the method of interview, the teachers' self reflecting competences, preferences, experiences, guidelines for cultural teaching, cultural contents and opinions on including culture in their lessons were to be found. Results from the interviews should complement the whole picture of the real situation of cultural teaching within English lessons in primary schools.

A semi-structured interview using an open-ended schedule was carried out with 51 English teachers from primary schools. All 30 observed teachers were interviewed after their lessons were observed. The aim was to gain extra information, but also to see if the teachers' declarations were a true reflection of their lessons. A further 21 English teachers from all over Slovakia were interviewed, to get additional information and to see if teachers from other parts of the country had different views and experiences. These teachers were randomly picked and interviewed at conferences and other meetings. They came from villages and towns from diverse locations across the country (e.g. Trenčín, Levice, Rožňava, Mlynky, Prievidza, Handlová, Trnava, Dubnica nad Váhom, Mankovce, etc).

For the analyses, a system of categories and codes was created based on the open-ended schedule used for the interviews. 6 categories were created and each category includes several codes. For a better illustration, the categories and codes can be viewed in the following table:

Category: 1. Knowledge of the English culture and ICC acquired:
Codes:
1. At University 2. In English speaking countries 3. Through Books, films 4. Through self-study 5. Other
Category: 2. Self reflection of the teachers (how good the teachers think their cultural knowledge and ICC are)
Codes:
1. Very good 2. Good 3. Weak
Category: 3. Periodicity of including cultural teaching into the English lessons
Codes:
1. Never 2. Occasionally (1–2 times a month) 3. Often (once a week or more)

Category: 4. Content of cultural teaching
Codes:
1. Information about the countries and places 2. Traditions, celebrations and festivals 3. History and literature 4. Film and music 5. Greeting phrases, introductions, positive and negative politeness, correct use of thank you, please, etc. 6. Phrases expressing agreement, disagreement, understanding 7. Comparisons of cultural aspects
Category: 5. Sources and guidelines for cultural teaching
Codes:
1. Curriculum 2. CEFR 3. School books 4. Other
Category: 6. Teachers' opinions on cultural teaching within English lessons
Codes:
1. Culture as an important part of language in all its aspects 2. Culture as an important part of language, but more as an additional 5th skill 3. Culture as a motivational aspect 4. Culture as an interesting aspect without much significance 5. Unnecessary chore 6. In addition, what teachers think of teaching culture within English language lessons

Table 14: Categories and codes for interview analyses

This system of categories and codes was applied to all 51 interviewed teachers. Each category is analysed separately first and then the chapter ends with a summary of the findings from all the categories and codes.

The first category "Knowledge of English culture and ICC" gives information about where the interviewed teachers obtained and developed their cultural knowledge and ICC (studies at universities, visits or stays in English speaking countries, reading books or watching films, self-studying and other sources). The codes were created from the questions from the open-ended schedule.

Code number 1 refers to the cultural knowledge and ICC obtained at universities. Out of 51 teachers, only 22 teachers claimed that they obtained their cultural knowledge and ICC during their studies at universities. However, only 14 teachers said that their knowledge and competences acquired at the universities was sufficient. The remaining 8 teachers reported that the knowledge and competences gained at the university was insufficient. Most of the teachers complained about the lack of native speakers and practical courses at universities. The alarming fact is that a total of 29 teachers out of 51 felt that university education was not offering them enough training in developing their cultural knowledge and ICC. This knowledge should be taken into consideration by teaching colleges in creating their study programmes.

Code number 2 refers to the cultural knowledge and ICC gained in an English speaking country. The amount of time spent in the particular country was also noted. 19 out of 51 teachers claimed that they gained cultural knowledge and ICC during their stays in an English speaking country. 4 out of the 19 teachers developed cultural knowledge and ICC from their occasional visits. 8 out of 19 teachers spent up to 2 years in an English speaking country while 7 out of 19 teachers spent more than 2 years in an English speaking country. 32 teachers did not address this code.

Code number 3 refers to the cultural knowledge and ICC obtained by reading books or watching films. 22 out of 51 teachers reported that they gained cultural knowledge of English speaking countries and ICC from reading books or watching films. 29 teachers did not mention this code.

Code number 4 shows the number of teachers who developed cultural knowledge and ICC through self-study. 24 out of 51 teachers mentioned this code as the main way of obtaining cultural knowledge and developing ICC. 27 teachers did not address this code.

Code number 5 refers to the open question about other possibilities of obtaining cultural knowledge and ICC. Only 5 out of 51 teachers answered this question and they named these other sources that helped them to gain and develop their cultural knowledge and ICC: the internet, friends, language schools, the news, English speaking people visiting their homes.

Teachers had a choice to answer more than one possibility, which most of them did. Most teachers (28) named two sources, 6 teachers named three sources and 1 teacher named four sources. The combination of sources varied greatly and could be generalized. 16 teachers selected only a single source for gaining cultural knowledge and ICC.

For a better illustration, the results are summarised in the following table:

Category: 1 Source of the knowledge of the English culture acquired:			
Codes:			
1. University	YES 22 teachers (out of 51) = 43%		NO 29 teachers (out of 51) = 57%
	14 teachers (out of 22) - sufficient = 64%	8 teachers (out of 22) - insufficient = 36%	
2. English speaking country	YES 19 teachers (out of 51) = 37%		NO 32 teachers (out of 51) = 63%
	4 (19) occasional	8 (19) up to 2 years / 7 (19) more than 2	
3. Books, films	YES 22 teachers (out of 51) = 43%		NO 29 teachers (out of 51) = 57%
4. Self-study	YES 24 teachers (out of 51) = 47%		NO 27 teachers (out of 51) = 53%
5. Other	5 teachers: the internet, friends, language schools, the news, English speaking people		

Table 15:   Knowledge of English culture and intercultural competences

The second category "Self reflection of the teachers" gives information about what the interviewed teachers thought of their own cultural knowledge and ICC. Three codes were based on the questions from the open-ended schedule. Most teachers, 36 out of 51, evaluated their knowledge and competences as good (code 2). 11 teachers out of 51 evaluated their knowledge and competences as weak (code 3) and 4 teachers out of 51 evaluated their cultural knowledge and ICC as very good (code 1). It is hard make any definitive conclusions based on the answers from these questions as the teachers were embarrassed to evaluate their own knowledge and competences and we must consider objectivity. It would be more objective to test the teachers' ICC directly, but the teachers felt reluctant to be tested due to the fear of a lack of anonymity in the results.

For a better illustration, the findings are summarised in the following table:

Category: 2 Self reflection of the teachers	(how good the teachers think their cultural knowledge and ICC are)
Codes:	
1. Very good	4 teachers (out of 51) = 8%
2. Good	36 teachers (out of 51) = 71%
3. Weak	11 teachers (out of 51) = 22%

Table 16:   Self reflection of the teachers

The third category "Periodicity of including cultural teaching in the English lessons" gives information on how often the interviewed English teachers included some cultural teaching in their lessons. 32 out of teachers 51 stated that they only occasionally (1–2 times a month) included cultural teaching in their lessons. The occasional involvement of cultural teaching refers to code number 2. These teachers identified the periodicity of their cultural teaching with the cultural pages in the school books, or with culturally connected topics, or with the festivals and traditions. 19 out of 51 teachers claimed that they included cultural teaching in their lessons often (once a week or more). This refers to code number 3. Most of these teachers said that they included some cultural aspects wherever possible or at every suitable occasion. None of the teachers referred to code number 1, which states that the periodicity of including cultural teaching is 'never'.

For a better illustration, the findings are summarised in the following table:

Category: 3 Periodicity of including cultural teaching in the English lessons	
Codes:	
1. Never 2. Occasionally (1–2 times a month) 3. Often (once a week or more)	0 teachers (out of 51) = 0% 32 teachers (out of 51) = 63% 19 teachers (out of 51) = 37%

Table 17:   Periodicity of including cultural teaching in the English lessons

The fourth category "Content of cultural teaching" provides information on which aspects of culture the interviewed teachers paid attention to, and which aspects they included in their lessons. The teachers were given a choice of the cultural aspects (codes), and were also asked to name examples of the aspects they selected.

Code number 1 refers to the content of "Information about the countries and places". 45 out of 51 teachers claimed that they included information about countries and places in their lessons. 6 teachers did not name what they included, but 39 teachers named examples: UK towns, places (London, Edinburgh), schools, uniforms, food and houses. Less frequent examples were: the USA, New York, sights, the royal family and geographical facts.

Code number 2 refers to the content of "Traditions, celebrations and festivals". All 51 teachers said that they included English traditions, celebrations and festivals in their lessons. They included them at the appropriate time of the year showing pupils pictures and talking about typical English traditions. All the teachers mentioned Halloween, Christmas and Easter, but some teachers also mentioned celebrations such as St. Patrick's Day, St. Valentine's Day and Pancake Tuesday.

Some teachers decorated their classrooms, sang songs, organized parties or prepared Christmas pudding.

Code number 3 deals with the content of "History and literature". 17 out of 51 teachers sought to include some aspects of history or literature in their lessons. Examples of historical aspects were quoted by only 3 teachers. Robin Hood was mentioned twice (a part of the school book) and one teacher also mentioned Queen Elizabeth I as a part of the contents of her cultural teaching. From literature, 12 teachers mentioned children's poems, fairy tales, Disney stories (one school book is entirely based on Disney stories), Harry Potter or the Mr. Men stories. One of the interviewed teachers regularly used the Mr. Men books, which she claimed to have had very good experiences with, as children love the stories and find them funny, but also educational. 2 teachers did not specify what they included in their lessons. It is believed that literary characters, children stories and some aspects of history are suitable and interesting subjects for teaching foreign languages and culture. However, from the interviews it was evident that most teachers did not involve any aspects of English literature or history, as they thought that it was too early for their pupils to work with such subject matter. I argue that these teachers' assumptions are wrong, as pupils often read Slovak translations of English books and they are interested in finding out and comparing, for example, the English names of characters, places, etc. I have also experienced with 3rd grade pupils (outside of this research), that pupils very much enjoy learning about the destruction of the Spanish Armada.

Code number 4 refers to the inclusion of "Film and music" in the English language lessons. 37 out of 51 teachers said that they used music or films during their language lessons. All 37 teachers used songs, but only 8 teachers used films. Most used songs for general language teaching and not particularly for cultural teaching. For cultural teaching, songs for Christmas, or Easter were used. Teachers also mentioned using songs from their school books, or a collection of English songs by the Slovak singer Miroslav Zbirka, or popular songs from youtube. From films, Marry Poppins and Alice in Wonderland were mentioned. Some teachers said that they occasionally talked with their pupils about new films. And some teachers said that they wanted to watch more films with their pupils, but that there was no time, or that they watched some films at the end of the school year.

Code number 5 refers to the inclusion of "greeting phrases, introductions, positive and negative politeness, correct use of thank you, please, etc." in the English language lessons. 44 out of teachers 51 claimed that they included at least some of these socio-cultural phrases into their teaching. When they were asked to give examples of some phrases they use with their pupils, as many as 18 teachers could not name any examples. Still, most teachers just referred to the phrases from the school books, or basic greetings and introductions. One teacher even admitted that she did not pay any attention to this topic. There was one teacher who gave an example of using "Pardon" in the meaning of "I'm sorry", which is evidently the wrong cultural use of this word (this is a false friend from the use of the Slovak expression). Proper use of the word "pardon" would be in phrases such as "Pardon me; I beg your pardon" meaning "Excuse me" or "I don't understand". Only 7 teachers said that they tried to use phrases regularly and gave examples such as "Bless you; Could you please…; Would you like…; Be so kind…; Here you are; You are welcome; Can I help you?; It's nice to see you; Excuse me; I'm sorry; etc.".

Code number 6 refers to the inclusion of "Phrases expressing agreement, disagreement, understanding" in the English lessons. 30 teachers claimed that they used these kinds of phrases in their lessons, but as many as 17 teachers did not give any examples of such phrases or referred to the phrases from the school books. Most teachers gave examples of phrases such as "Do you understand?; I don't understand.". Only 4 teachers gave some more examples of phrases such as "What does it mean?; It's ok.; Do you agree?; What do you think?; Is it clear?".

Code number 7 deals with "Comparisons of cultural aspects" during the English lessons. 38 teachers stated that they compared cultural aspects, mainly traditions (23 teachers), schools (10 teachers), food (3 teachers), or houses and towns. 8 teachers did not specify which subjects of culture they compared. One teacher said that she did that with older pupils, but not the younger ones.

For a better illustration, the findings are summarised in the following table:

Category: 4. Content of cultural teaching		
Codes:		
1. Information about the countries and places	45 teachers (out of 51) = 88%	UK towns, places, schools, uniforms, houses, food, USA, royal family, etc.
2. Traditions, celebrations and festivals	51 teachers (out of 51) = 100%	Halloween, Christmas, Easter, St. Patrick's Day, Valentines Day, Pancake Tuesday
3. History and literature	17 teachers (out of 51) = 33%	Robin Hood, fairy tales, Harry Potter, Mr. Men, Disney stories, etc.
4. Film and music	37 teachers (out of 51) = 73%	Easter, Christmas songs, Marry Poppins, Alice in Wonderland

Category: 4. Content of cultural teaching		
5. greeting phrases, introductions, positive and negative politeness, correct use of thank you, please, etc.	44 teachers (out of 51) = 86% 7 teachers (out of 51) gave examples = 14%	Bless you; Could you please…; Would you like…; Be so kind…; Here you are; You are welcome; Can I help you?; It's nice to see you; Excuse me; I'm sorry; etc.
6. Phrases expressing agreement, disagreement, understanding	30 teachers (out of 51) = 59% 4 teachers (out of 51) gave examples = 8%	I don't understand, I understand; What does it mean?; It's ok.; Do you agree?; What do you think?; Is it clear?
7. Comparisons of cultural aspects	38 teachers (out of 51) = 75%	Traditions, schools, food, houses, towns

Table 18:   Content of cultural teaching

The fifth category "Sources and guidelines for cultural teaching" provides information on where the interviewed teachers got their guidance from and which sources they used for cultural teaching. The teachers were asked to name which curricular documents, or school books they extracted their guidance from, or to name any other sources and guidelines. More than one choice was welcome.

Code number 1 refers to the use of the Curriculum as a guideline for cultural teaching. 35 out of 51 teachers claimed to use the Curriculum as a guide for their cultural teaching. Code number 2 refers to the use of the CEFR as a guideline for cultural teaching. Only 8 out of 51 teachers made reference to use of the CEFR. Code number 3 specifies schools books as guidance material for cultural teaching. 33 out of 51 teachers referred to the use of school books as the source for their cultural teaching. 49 teachers also named other sources (such as the internet, other books, magazines), which are represented in code number 4. Most teachers specified more than one source for their cultural teaching, only 2 teachers specified one source, and 3 teachers referred to all four codes.

For a better illustration, the findings are summarised in the following table:

Category: 5. Sources and guidelines for cultural teaching	
Codes:	
5. Curriculum	35 teachers (out of 51) = 69%
6. CEFR	8 teachers (out of 51) = 16%
7. School books	33 teachers (out of 51) = 65%
8. Other	49 teachers (internet, books, magazines) = 96%

Table 19:   Sources and guidelines for cultural teaching

The sixth category "Teachers' opinions on cultural teaching within English language lessons" offers insight into what the interviewed teachers thought about the importance of cultural teaching within English language lessons. Teachers were given a choice of five statements, from which they could select more than one which they agreed with. There was an additional sixth question, which was open to the teachers to add their own opinions on implementing cultural teaching in their lessons.

Code number 1 refers to the statement "Culture as an important part of language in all its aspects", and only 16 out of 51 teachers chose this statement. Code number 2 refers to the statement "Culture as an important part of language, but more as an additional 5th skill", and 20 out of 51 teachers chose this statement. Most teachers, 38 out of 51 chose the statement "Culture as a motivational aspect" (code 3), but usually combined with another statement (code 1 or 2). 8 out of 51 teachers chose code number 4, which is represented by the statement "Culture as an interesting aspect without much significance". No teachers referred to code number 5 "Unnecessary chore".

30 out of 51 teachers expressed their opinions in code number 6 "In addition, what teachers think about teaching culture within English language lessons". Many answers stated that cultural aspects inspire pupils to learn the foreign language and to visit the target country, and it generally broadens their general knowledge. Some of the teachers referred to having experienced great interest from the side of the pupils, and that the pupils wanted to learn and see the differences between their culture and that of the target language. They stated that the students made comments and expressed surprise. One teacher said that her pupils were enthusiastically participating in a project called "Flat Friends" (106 pupils), which involved corresponding with English children and in this way learning about their culture. Quite a number of teachers complained about the lack of time to include cultural teaching in their lessons. They objected to the teaching plans being very limited, and that the plans gave teachers no scope for

any other activities. One teacher expressed an opinion on other teachers, that they may be lazy or unwilling to include teaching cultural aspects in their lessons. Furthermore, two teachers stated that in their opinion, teaching culture to primary school pupils is not suitable, as the pupils do not show any interest or understand the cultural issues.

For a better illustration, the findings are summarised in the following table:

Category: 6. Teachers' opinions on cultural teaching within English language lessons	
Codes:	
1. Culture as an important part of language in all its aspects	teachers (out of 51) = 31%
2. Culture as an important part of language, but more as an additional 5th skill	teachers (out of 51) = 39%
3. Culture as a motivational aspect	38 teachers (out of 51) = 75%
4. Culture as an interesting aspect without much significance	8 teachers (out of 51) = 16%
5. Unnecessary chore	0 teachers
6. In addition, what teachers think of teaching culture within English language lessons	30 teachers (Culture: inspirational, motivational, important factor, broadens general knowledge, teachers' complains about the lack of time, not suitable for young learners)

Table 20: Teachers' opinions on cultural teaching within English language lessons

4.3.1. Conclusion of the interview analyses

The aim of the interview analyses was to study and interpret information given by 51 teachers, who were interviewed about teaching culture in English language lessons at primary schools. By analyzing, comparing and looking for parallels or clashes we intended to find out, as real as possible, a view on teaching culture in the English language lessons. All 30 observed teachers and a further 21 teachers from all around Slovakia were interviewed. 6 main categories, each including several codes were created for the analyses. We analysed each category individually above. For a better illustration, all the categories and codes are summarized in the following table:

Category: 1. Source of the knowledge of the English culture and intercultural competences acquired:	
Codes:	
1. University	22 teachers (out of 51) = 43%
2. English speaking country	19 teachers (out of 51) = 37%
3. Books, films	22 teachers (out of 51) = 43%
4. Self study	24 teachers (out of 51) = 47%
5. Other	5 teachers (internet, friends, language schools, news, English people)
Category: 2. Self reflection of the teachers (how good the teachers think their cultural knowledge and intercultural communicative competences are)	
Codes:	
1. Very good	4 teachers (out of 51) = 8%
2. Good	36 teachers (out of 51) = 71%
3. Weak	11 teachers (out of 51) = 22%
Category: 3. Periodicity of including cultural teaching in the English lessons	
Codes:	
1. Never	0 teachers (out of 51) = 0%
2. Occasionally (1–2 times a month)	32 teachers (out of 51) = 63%
3. Often (once a week or more)	19 teachers (out of 51) = 37%
Category: 4. Content of cultural teaching	
Codes:	
1. Information about the countries and places	45 teachers (out of 51) = 88%
2. Traditions, celebrations and festivals	52 teachers (out of 51) = 100%
	17 teachers (out of 51) = 33%
3. History and literature	37 teachers (out of 51) = 73%
4. Film and music	44 teachers (out of 51) = 86%
5. Greeting phrases, introductions, positive and negative politeness, correct use of thank you, please, etc.	7 teachers (out of 51) gave examples = 14%
	30 teachers (out of 51) = 59%
6. Phrases expressing agreement, disagreement, understanding	4 teachers (out of 51) gave examples = 8%
7. Comparisons of cultural aspects	38 teachers (out of 51) = 75%

Category: 5. Sources and guidelines for cultural teaching	
Codes:	
1. Curriculum	35 teachers (out of 51) = 69%
CEFR	8 teachers (out of 51) = 16%
2. School book	33 teachers (out of 51) = 65%
3. Other	49 teachers (internet, books, magazines)
Category: 6. Teachers' opinions on cultural teaching within English lessons	
Codes:	
1. Culture as an important part of language in all its aspects	teachers (out of 51) = 31%
	teachers (out of 51) = 39%
2. Culture as an important part of language, but more as an additional 5th skill	38 teachers (out of 51) = 75%
	8 teachers (out of 51) = 16%
3. Culture as a motivational aspect	0 teachers
4. Culture as an interesting aspect without much significance	30 teachers (Culture: inspirational, motivational, important factor, broadens
5. Unnecessary chore	general knowledge, teachers' complains
6. In addition, what teachers think of teaching culture within English language lessons	about the lack of time, not suitable for young learners)

Table 21:   Summary of interview analyses

To summarize the interview analyses, the research questions have to be answered.

Research question number 2 (from the further research questions) states:

"Where do the Slovak teachers get guidance and information for their cultural teaching?"

- Most teachers (49 = 96%) chose the 'other sources' and they stated to mainly use the internet, but also other books and magazines as sources and guidelines for their cultural teaching.
- The Curriculum was chosen by 35 (69%) teachers.
- 33 teachers (65%) use school books as the source materials for their cultural teaching.
- The CEFR was chosen only by 8 teachers (16%), which is deemed to be disappointing because the CEFR provides the most complete information on teaching foreign languages.
- However, most teachers named more than one source or guideline for the source of their cultural teaching, mainly combining the Curriculum, school books and other sources.

Research question number 3 (from the further research questions) states:
   "Which aspects of culture do English teachers in Slovakia prefer to teach?"

- All 51 teachers (100%) declared they teach traditions, celebrations and festivals.
- 45 teachers (88%) stated they included factual information on countries and places in their lessons.
- 38 teachers (75%) said that they compared cultural aspects such as traditions, schools and food during their lessons.
- 37 teachers (73%) reported to use music or films during their lessons, but most of them used songs for general language teaching and not cultural teaching.
- 17 teachers (33%) said that they included some history or literature in their lessons, mainly fairy tales and children's poems.
- Overall, the above mentioned aspects belong in the visible part of the cultural iceberg (socio-cultural knowledge). Generally these visible aspects of culture were referred to frequently by teachers, and the teachers were able to give many examples of them within the content of their cultural teaching.
- Quite a different situation became apparent concerning the invisible part of the cultural iceberg. Two questions were created concerning socio-cultural and pragmatic phrases (code 5, 6). Even though as many as 44 teachers (86%) reported to teach and use the socio-cultural phrases (code 5) in their lessons, most of the teachers (37) could not name examples of such phrases, or gave extremely basic examples, without much cultural connotation. A similar situation occurred concerning the pragmatic phrases (code 6), where 30 teachers (59%) claimed to teach and use them, but again most of the teachers (26) could not name examples of such phrases.
- To conclude this research question, it is apparent that most teachers preferred to teach aspects of the visible part of the cultural iceberg, such as traditions, celebrations, festivals, factual information on countries and places, and songs. Unfortunately the aspects from the invisible part of the cultural iceberg are largely underestimated, or the importance of them is misunderstood.

Research question number 4 (from the further research questions) states:
   "How do the Slovak teachers reflect on their own intercultural communicative competence?"

- Most interviewed teachers (36 teachers = 71%) evaluated their own cultural knowledge and intercultural competences as good.
- 11 teachers (22%) stated that their cultural knowledge and intercultural competences were weak.

- Only 4 teachers (8%) regarded their cultural knowledge and intercultural competences as very good.
- As stated earlier, it was difficult to perceive objectivity from the answers, as the interviewed teachers felt uneasy to evaluate their own knowledge and competences. However, a degree of objectivity could be found with some teachers, when comparing information from the first category referring to where the teachers acquired their knowledge of English culture and intercultural competences, and the second category self-evaluating ones' own competences. Three out of the four teachers who claimed to have very good cultural knowledge and competences spent more than 3 years in an English speaking country, so the outcome of very good intercultural competence was expected. At the other end of the scale, 10 out of 11 teachers who claimed to have weak cultural knowledge and intercultural competences stated that they did not obtain their cultural knowledge and competences at their universities, and that the university courses were unsatisfactory. It is alarming that 30 out of 51 teachers perceive university courses unsatisfactory, or not good at developing cultural knowledge and ICC for future English language teachers.

4.4. Conclusion and discussion of the research – Triangulation

The main aim of this research was to identify, analyse and explain theoretically what and how cultural aspects are taught in English language lessons in primary education in Slovakia (A1 level according to the CEFR). The aim was to find out the extent, contents, methods, techniques and materials used for developing the pupils' intercultural communicative competence.

To be able to capture such a holistic view on teaching culture within English language lessons, a qualitative research design was chosen for this study. Three naturalistic research methods - documentary analyses, observation and interviews - were used to explore different views of the same phenomenon: teaching cultural aspects within English language lessons. I have already analysed and made conclusions from each research method individually, but what still needs to be done is to inter-relate, combine, and look for parallels or clashes between all three research methods, to complete the whole picture.

The document analyses were a considerable part of the research, as two Slovak curricula (pre-reform and current) and the CEFR (which was chosen as the reference document) were analysed and compared. The aim was to find out the extent of the cultural content in both curricula, to compare them, and see if there was an improvement in the current Slovak curriculum relating to the development of ICC. The findings reveal that the current curriculum included less than a third (29%) of the set 28 codes concerning cultural aspects, which is considered as highly unsatisfactory. In particular, the missing aspects regarding negative politeness, exclamations, living conditions, social conventions, non-verbal communication, recommended materials, methods and techniques should have been included in the curriculum. Comparing the two Slovak curricular documents, there was not an obvious positive or negative shift between the pre-reform and current curriculum, only some aspects were elaborated upon in a better manner in both the pre-reform or the current curriculum. For example, the current curriculum paid more attention to the development of certain socio-linguistic and pragmatic competences, but less attention to the socio-cultural knowledge.

The method of observation can be considered as the most crucial research method in the current study, as the most valuable information was gained through observation. The most astonishing finding was that less than half (48%) of the observed lessons included cultural aspects, even though all the teachers were informed prior to their lesson observation about the aim of the research, and were asked to include some cultural teaching in their lessons. A great majority (85%) of the lessons which included cultural aspects paid attention to the visible parts of the cultural iceberg, in other words acquiring socio-cultural knowledge. However, only 17% of the lessons included invisible parts of the cultural iceberg (sociolinguistic and pragmatic competences), which are undoubtedly an integral element of successful intercultural communication. No single lesson included paralinguistic competences. The most common material for teaching culture was the "cultural pages" from a school book, which was used in more than half of the lessons (54%). Also non-authentic and authentic materials were used at about a third of the lessons (38%). Only 8 lessons included a combination of different materials. Nonetheless, it is important how the materials are used during a lesson. Even the "cultural pages" from a school book can be incorporated within a lesson in a gripping fashion. However what was observed in most of the lessons, is that the texts were just read, translated, or listened to from a CD without any deeper appreciation, or understanding of the cultural issues. This is, in reality, a missed opportunity to convey cultural knowledge to the pupils. But authentic materials can also appear boring to the students, if they are only exhibited to the pupils without being used in the form of an activity for example. In a positive light, generally any authentic or non-authentic materials were perceived by the pupils with much more interest, and especially authentic materials viewed as "the real English things".

It was observed, that pupils were the most engaged during the lessons, where authentic materials were used in role plays or games. Comparison, discussions, explanations and completing exercises were the most frequent techniques used for cultural teaching. To a lesser extent, role plays, projects, noticing, games and the concept of a cultural island were used. Mainly one technique was used whereas only five times a combination of two or more techniques was used. Sadly, overall most teachers used uninteresting techniques for cultural teaching, and only a few used techniques which visibly gripped the pupils' attention. Unfortunately out of the 50 observed lessons, only a few fulfilled the criteria for an effective lesson concerning the development of intercultural communicative competences. This indicates that teachers need coaching on how to best incorporate cultural elements into their lessons, as it cannot be expected to occur naturally.

The third supplementary method in the current research was the interview. All the observed teachers, plus additional teachers, were interviewed about the implementation of cultural teaching in their lessons. The teachers were asked about the sources of their knowledge, their preferences, experiences, guidelines, opinions, but also to evaluate their own intercultural communicative competences. Most teachers (69%) named two, three or even more sources of their cultural knowledge and intercultural competences. The most frequent sources or ways of obtaining cultural knowledge and competences were through self-study (47%), books and films (43%), university courses (43%), stays in an English speaking country (37%), but also the internet, friends, the news and language schools. From the teachers who mentioned universities as places of obtaining cultural knowledge and competences, only 27% found the university courses as satisfactory in this respect. It is staggering, that so many teachers think that universities do not provide sufficient courses for the development of the intercultural communicative competences of their students. Almost three quarters (71%) of the interviewed teachers evaluated their own cultural knowledge and intercultural competences as good, one fifth (22%) as weak and only 8% as very good. Three out of the four teachers who claimed to have very good cultural knowledge and competences gained their knowledge and competences during extended stays in an English speaking country. This outcome is to be expected, as it is quite logical and natural in the process of adaptation in a foreign country, to get accustomed with the values, beliefs and ways of behaviour of the representatives of the particular culture. Most of the teachers who obtained cultural knowledge and competences during their stays in an English speaking country claimed to include cultural aspects in their lessons at least once a week. However 63% of the teachers included cultural aspects only occasionally (1–2 a month) and their cultural teaching was usually connected with the "cultural pages" in the school books. There were also teachers who admitted that they did "cultural pages" only if there was enough time left over, otherwise they skipped them. Most teachers (69%) got their guidance from the Curriculum. 65% of teachers used school books as guideline sources and only 16% used the CEFR. Almost all the teachers (96%) stated they use the internet, magazines or other books as sources of their cultural teaching. Only 31% of the interviewed teachers viewed cultural teaching as an important part of language education in all its aspects, 37% as an extra 5th skill and 16% as an interesting aspect without much significance. As many as 75% of the teachers thought of cultural teaching as motivational. All the teachers claimed to teach traditions, celebrations and festivals. Factual information, children's stories and songs were reasonably common contents of cultural teaching. Even though many teachers claimed to include phrases of sociolinguistic and pragmatic competences in their lessons, not many teachers were able to name examples of such phrases. Overall, it became clear that most teachers paid attention to the visible part of the cultural iceberg and the invisible part of the cultural iceberg was either underestimated or unappreciated.

The individual methods give us valuable information and offer us insight into the matter of cultural teaching within English language lessons. However, by triangulation we can gain the whole picture; see associations or even contradictions between the collected data from individual research methods. Triangulation of the three methods also increases the validity of the data.

As I have come to the conclusion about the pre-reform and current curriculum being unsatisfactory concerning cultural aspects, it was expected that this would have an impact on the teachers and their lessons. The fact that only less than half of the observed lessons included cultural aspects only affirms my prediction. The biggest observed contradiction was between the data from the observations and interviews. All the interviewed teachers claimed to teach cultural aspects at least once a month, but only 16 out of 30 observed teachers included cultural teaching in their lessons, even though they were asked to do so. I assume that they did not really understand what cultural teaching meant, and as the interview was conducted afterwards, probably the interview schedule consisted of questions prompting positive responses to the aspect of cultural content. Another example of teachers not knowing the meaning of cultural teaching were two notable lessons, which included the use of socio-cultural and pragmatic phrases. One teacher implemented such phrases naturally into applicable situations and the other teacher into a shopping role play. Neither of these two teachers was aware of developing pupils' intercultural communicative competences. From both the observation and interviews, it was obvious that teachers who spent considerable time in an English speaking country tended to implement cultural teaching in their lessons more often and more effectively, even though they were not always aware that they were doing so. It is believed that it is because they experienced first-hand the importance of intercultural communication, and felt the necessity to teach cultural aspects to their pupils. The finding that such a great number of teachers were not satisfied with the university courses concerning cultural teaching complements the observation that not many teachers understood the meaning of cultural teaching. Also the general belief that culture is represented by traditions, celebrations, facts about countries, places and people is reflected in the data gained from both observation and interviews, as these visible parts of the cultural iceberg were by-and-large more prevalent in the observed lessons and also in the interviews.

From the current study it is quite clear that English teachers have problems with teaching cultural aspects at a primary school level in Slovakia. It is most likely that one of the reasons why they have problems with teaching culture is that they do not receive adequate education in the area of intercultural communication. As a consequence, teachers do not know how to teach cultural aspects, even though they believe they do. As the teachers' problems in reaching goals related to teaching culture are systemic and cultural, subsequently it requires more complex research.

It can be concluded, that if universities do not provide good quality courses for intercultural communication, teachers will not really know what is included in the aspects of culture, and will not realize the importance of cultural awareness, knowledge and intercultural competences in order to communicate successfully with the representatives of different cultures. Most teachers rely on the curriculum as the main guideline for their teaching. If the curriculum does not offer properly explained and well-structured guidelines concerning all the important aspects of language, teachers cannot be expected to know and conduct excellent lessons which include all aspects of the language. Successful cultural teaching is a result of both: good university courses, which should provide future teachers with substantial knowledge of culture and intercultural communication, plus methodological facilities for the development of intercultural communicative competences of the pupils, and extensive information in the curriculum on intercultural teaching, materials and methods. As a result of these two conditions (curriculum, university courses) being unsatisfactory in this aspect, it appears that most teachers are often confused or unaware of what and how cultural elements should be included within English language lessons, with the aim of developing intercultural communicative competences. If possible, students and teachers should spend more time in English speaking countries, as encounters with native speakers, but also representatives of different cultures, provide the most natural way of gaining intercultural communicative competences. However travelling abroad is not always easily achievable mainly because of financial reasons, so at least encouraging having foreign lecturers at schools and universities would be a limited, but advantageous option, for intercultural communication.

4.5. Implications and recommendations for linguo-didactics

Based on the results of the current research, several proposals are provided for improving undergraduate teacher training programs, practice of English language teachers and finally suggestions for further language pedagogy research.

4.5.1. Recommendations for teacher training programs

In order to improve teachers' ICC, it is recommended for the faculties of education to:

- improve the existing subjects, such as: the Culture of English speaking countries and British and American studies. Apart from teaching historical and factual information, to emphasize the inclusion of socio-cultural, pragmatic and paralinguistic competences, especially those which are typical for the target culture and different from our own culture,
- offer a new subject: Intercultural communication to English teacher trainees, where they could acquire knowledge on culture, the relationship between language and culture, intercultural communication, intercultural competences and intercultural communicative competences. Practicing intercultural activities (identification and solution of intercultural misunderstandings, role plays, problem solving, drama, etc.) would be beneficial for developing students' ICC, which would, as a consequence, reflect in their teaching practice,
- include a new section on teaching culture within the aforementioned existing subjects mentioned in point one and two, or in the subject Methodology of teaching English. The teacher trainees would learn how to develop the ICC of pupils of different ages and language proficiency.

4.5.2. Recommendations for Continued Professional Development (CPD) of English language teachers

- existing teachers should not vigorously follow just the school books, but should also include authentic and also non-authentic materials in order to make lessons more interesting, to inspire pupils and to bring authenticity into their English language lessons,

- existing teachers should continue (after graduating) to improve their ICC by means of participation in workshops, methodical seminars and conferences at home or abroad, e.g. within a Programme of CPD of English language teachers,
- teachers should read literature and studies, from which they can learn about new research and trends in teaching culture within English language lessons and get inspiration for their own teaching,
- teachers should maintain contact with the most up to date situations in English speaking countries by following the news, reading English speaking newspapers, magazines, spending time with native speakers and travelling to English speaking countries.

4.5.3. Recommendations for further language pedagogy research

- elaboration of a collection of techniques and activities for the development of ICC
- based on the outcomes of document analyses from the current research, it is recommended for the national curriculum to be amended and brought into line with the CEFR (socio-cultural, sociolinguistic, pragmatic, paralinguistic competences, recommended materials and methods for teaching cultural aspects within English language lessons).

Conclusion

One of the priorities of European Union is to equip modern European citizens with the abilities to communicate effectively across linguistic and cultural boundaries in multicultural and multilingual Europe. In order to fulfil these needs, European citizens have to be interculturally communicatively competent. This was the main reason for conducting the current research, which investigated how ICCs are developed within English language lessons in Slovak primary schools. The aim of the research was to specifically identify, analyse and compare the intercultural contents in the Slovak curricula and English language lessons in primary schools in Slovakia. Three curricular documents were analysed, actual English language lessons observed and English language teachers interviewed concerning the extent, content, methods, techniques and materials used for developing the pupils' ICC. By triangulation of methods, the findings from individual methods were compared for parallels, clashes and supplemented with additional information.

The monograph began by stating the research problem, including specific research aims and questions, where one main aim and three further subsequent research aims were set. Three research questions were created with regard to the main research aim and these were supplemented by four further research questions.

The theoretical element of the study provided a considerable foundation for the current research. The concepts and role of culture within English language education were analysed and discussed. The Common European Framework for Languages (2001) was included and analysed as it serves as a model for creating national curricula in the European countries and it promotes ICC as one of the key competences. Many scholars' views on the implementation of an intercultural perspective within English language lessons were presented. It can be generalized that most scholars considered culture as inseparable in foreign language education (Byram, 1989, 1997; Dunnett, Dubin, Lezberg, 1986; Kramsch, 1993, 1998; Brooks, 2001; Cullen, 2000; Straub, 1999; Robinson, 1988; Huhn, 1978). The findings from the current research prove the need to include culture in every aspect of foreign language learning, as foreign language teachers often treat culture as an additional and not always a necessary skill. Considerable time was devoted to the various methods, techniques and materials for teaching culture, which were collected and discussed with relation to their suitability.

The second chapter concludes with studies from the current research in the area of intercultural communication within ELT. Most research was carried out with international adult students abroad and their experiences with intercultural communication.

From the studies analysed, there has only been limited research carried out on cultural teaching within foreign language education at primary schools. Most of the research has been done with adults and has focused on their acquisition, abilities and experiences with intercultural communication. However, the research carried out by Europublic (2007), Zerzová (2012) and Kostková (2012) dealt with very similar issues and certain aspects can be compared to the current research, by which the validity can be enhanced. The outcomes show very similar results even though they were carried out independently in different environments.

Europublic (2007) completed a study for the European Commission on the intercultural skills taught in foreign language lessons in primary and lower secondary education in 12 European countries. Even though the Europublic (ibid.) study did not include Slovakia, the current research came to similar conclusions. The Europublic (ibid.) findings reported that the national curricula paid most attention to the development of linguistic competences and communication skills, and the ICC (if included) got paid considerably less attention. The current research revealed that the Slovak national curriculum included less than a third of the cultural aspects recommended by CEFR, which is considered as highly unsatisfactory. Most interviewed teachers in the Europublic (ibid.) study complained about the lack of time for including intercultural teaching in their lessons and about the missing guidance for teachers with regard to the development of ICC. Many teachers said that they would need more training for a better understanding of ICC, and that their previous teacher training was inadequate. In the current study three quarters of the interviewed teachers said that their cultural knowledge and ICC acquired at the universities were insufficient. Most of the teachers complained about the lack of native speakers and practical courses at the universities. Recommendations for educational practice are quite similar too: making ICC development alongside foreign language learning a key feature for multilingualism; improving teacher education concerning ICC; improving foreign language curricula in a way to include clearer and more detailed specifications of objectives, descriptions of didactic and methodological approaches and methods.

Zerzová (2012) dealt with the development of ICC within English language lessons at a lower secondary school education level in the Czech Republic. Very similar results can be found between the current research and Zerzová's research concerning cultural teaching and the cultural contents in the curricula. Both studies remarked that the national curricula talk generally about the importance of ICC, but do not specify how to develop them. Observation was a research method used in both studies. The Czech study reported that 62% of English lessons included cultural teaching while the current study reported 52% in the case of Slovakia; both being quite low. 100% of Czech and 85% of Slovak observed lessons paid attention to the development of the cognitive level (knowledge) of ICC, with behavioural and affective levels of ICC being neglected. The most common methods in teaching culture were the same in both countries: discussion, lecturing, pair work, individual work, role plays and games. The outcomes from both studies illustrated a great neglect of cultural teaching in schools in the Czech Republic and Slovakia.

Kostková's (2012) research included analyses of the Czech national curriculum and school curricula. She found out that the curricula did not sufficiently cover the development of ICC. The development of ICC was included only on a general basis and the curricula did not offer sufficient support for language teachers. In comparison, the Slovak national curriculum (2011) was also very superficially written with unsatisfactory contents of cultural aspects. Most Slovak teachers relied on the national curriculum as a guideline for their teaching, however the Slovak national curricula did not offer well elaborated guidelines and it could not be expected for teachers to conduct excellent lessons developing the ICC of their pupils. Kostková (ibid.) also pointed out that there is a need to create a subject, which would be didactically preparing teachers on how to develop the ICC of their learners within English language lessons. Similarly, in the current research the findings show that the interviewed teachers were not satisfied with their teacher training concerning ICC and the researcher's suggestions are to provide efficient courses at teacher training universities with the aim of preparing future teachers with a substantial knowledge of culture and ICC, plus methodological facilities for the development of the ICC of their learners.

The third chapter presented the whole research. A detailed description of the methodology of the research was provided. Individual methods: documentary analyses, observations and interviews were analysed and adapted for the current research. It was decided to triangulate the three methods used to compare and contrast the results. Issues concerning validity and reliability were addressed with much care and information on sampling, research subjects and the stages of research were also included.

The document analyses subchapter followed with a detailed elaboration of the three curricular documents: the Common European Framework for Languages: Learning, Teaching, Assessment A1 level (CERF, 2001), the Slovak pre-reform

English curriculum for the primary school level (2001) and the current Slovak national curriculum for the English language ISCED 1 (2011). The aim was to explore and compare the Slovak curricular documents (the pre-reform and current curriculum) with the Common European Framework for Languages (a reference document). The findings showed that the current curriculum included less than a third of set cultural aspects (based on CEFR) which is considered as insufficient. A positive shift was noticed in development of competences, but a negative shift in the area of socio-cultural knowledge.

The observation analyses subchapter interpreted the data gathered from the observation of English language lessons at primary schools. The aim was to outline the real situation in terms of implementing cultural aspects within English language lessons in primary schools in Slovakia. A lot of data were gained from the observations, but the most astonishing finding was that less than a half of the observed lessons included cultural aspects, even though all the teachers were informed about the aim of the research and were asked to include some cultural teaching in their lessons.

The interview analyses subchapter interpreted the data gained from the interviews with English language teachers. The aim was to find out teachers' preferences, experiences, opinions, self-reflections on competences and guidelines for their cultural teaching. From the interviews additional data considering the implementation of cultural aspects in English language lessons were gathered. It was revealed, that most teachers included socio-cultural knowledge (visible parts of the cultural iceberg) in their lessons and the invisible aspects (sociolinguistic, pragmatic and paralinguistic) they either neglected or did not realize their importance in the process of acquiring intercultural communicative competences.

Research conclusions were presented in the triangulation subchapter, where the findings from all three methods of research were brought together and discussed collectively to flesh out a fuller, more complete picture of the teaching of cultural aspects in the ELT classroom. It was concluded that many teachers did not know what cultural aspects comprise of and did not understand the importance of acquiring intercultural communicative competences. Most teachers relied on the curriculum as the main guideline for their teaching. If the curriculum did not offer properly explained guidelines concerning all the important elements of language, it could not be expected for teachers to know and conduct excellent lessons including all aspects of the language.

The final part of the third chapter offered recommendations for linguo-didactics. The proposals were divided into three categories: recommendations for undergraduate teacher training programs, recommendations for English language teachers and recommendations for further language pedagogical research.

The topic of intercultural communicative competences is relevant in today's multicultural and multilingual world. The aims of the current research concerning the implementation of cultural aspects in English language lessons were fulfilled. However, the topic of intercultural communication, intercultural competences and intercultural communicative competences is so vast, that continued future research into the subject would be of great benefit.

Bibliography

AIFTINCA, M. 2001. *Culture and Freedom*. Washington: The council for Research in Values and Philosophy, 2001. ISBN: 1565181360.

AFS INTL. 1984. *Afs orientation Handbook: 004*. Intercultural Pr, 1984. ISBN: 9995098989.

ALLEN, W.W. 1985. Toward cultural proficiency. In: Omaggio, A. C. (ed.) *Proficiency, Curriculum, Articulation: The Ties that Blind*. Middlebury, VT: Northeast Conference, 1985. ISBN: 978–0915432851.

ANDERSEN, M., TAYLOR, H. 2001. *Sociology: Understanding a Diverse Society*. Wadsworth Publishing Co Inc. 2001. ISBN: 978–0534587345.

ANDREW, M. 2011. *Reshaping educational experience by volunteering in the community: Language learners in the real world*. Journal of Intercultural Communication, ISSN 1404–1634, issue 25, March 2011. [online]. [cit. 12. 8. 2011]. Available on the internet: URL: http://www.immi.se/intercultural/.

ARASARATNAM, L.A. 2009. *The Development of a New Instrument of Intercultural Communication Competence*. Journal of Intercultural Communication, ISSN 1404–1634, issue 20, May 2009. [online]. [cit. 12. 8. 2011]. Available on the internet: http://www.immi.se/intercultural/.

BAKER, W. 2003. *Should culture be an overt component of EFL instruction outside of English speaking countries? The Thai context*. Asian EFL Journal, ISSN 1738–1460. [online]. [cit. 12. 8. 2011]. Available on the internet: http://www.asian-efl-journal.com/dec_03_sub.wb.php. 2003.

BEACCO, J.-C., BOUQUET, S., PORQUIER, R. 2004. Un Referentiel: Textes ET References Niveau B2 Pour Le Francais/Livre - Conseil urope. Didier, 2004. ISBN: 978–2278056118.

BERRY, J. W. 1980. Acculturation as varieties of adaptation. In A. Padilla (Ed.) Acculturation*: Theory, models and findings* (p. 9–25). Advancement of Science. 1980. ISBN: 978–0891588597.

BERRY, J.W. 2010. Cross-Cultural Psychology. In: Průcha, J. *Interkulturní komunikace*. Grada Publishing, 2010. ISBN: 9788024730691.

BERRY, J.W., POORTINGA, Y.H., BRUEGELMANS, S., CHASIOTIS, A., SAM, D.L. 2011. *Cross-Cultural Psychology*. 3rd Edition. New York: Cambridge University Press. 2011. ISBN: 978–0521745208.

125

BERRY, J. W., POORTINGA, Y. H., SEGALL, M. H. DASEN, P. R. 2002. *Cross-Cultural Psychology: Research and Applications.* Cambridge University Press. 2002. ISBN: 0521646170.

BERRY, J.,W., KIM, U., POWER, S., YOUNG, M., BUJAKI, M. 1989. In: Deardoff, D., K. 2009. *The SAGE Handbook of Intercultural Competence.* Sage Publications. ISBN: 1412960452.

BOAS, E. 1986. Language and thought. In: Valdes, M. (ed.) *Bridging the Cultural Gap in Language Teaching.* Cambridge: Cambridge University Press, 1986. ISBN: 978–0521310451.

BOAS, E. 2010. *The Mind of Primitive Man. Lulu.com.* 2010. ISBN: 978–0557368648.

BOLEDOVIČOVÁ, M. 2000. *Metodológia výskumu v ošetrovateľstve.* Dissertation work. Trnava: Trnavská univerzita. 2000.

BRINTON, D., WONG, A. 2003. *Authentic Materials Guide.* [online]. [cit.17.5.2010]. Available on the internet: http://www.lmp.ucla.edu/Lessons. aspx?menu=003. 2003.

BROOKS, N. 2001. Culture in the Classroom. In:. In: Valdes, M. (ed.) *Bridging the Cultural Gap in Language Teaching.* Cambridge: Cambridge University Press, 2001. ISBN: 0521310458.

BYRAM, M., MORGAN, C. et al. 1994. *Teaching and Learning Language and Culture.* Great Britain: WBC. 1994.

BYRAM, M. 1998. *Cultural Studies in Foreign Language Education.* Clevedon: Multilingual Matters, 1998. ISBN: 1853590177.

BYRAM, M. 1997. *Teaching and Assessing Intercultural Communicative Competence.* Clevedon, Philadellphia: Multilingual Matters, 1997. ISBN: 185359377.

BYRAM, M., BUTTJES, D. 1991. *Mediating Languages and Cultures: Towards an Intercultural Theory of Foreign Language Education.* Clevedon: Multilingual Matters, 1991. ISBN: 1853590703.

BYRAM, M., ESARTE-SARRIES, V., TAYLOR, S. 1991. *Cultural Studies and Language Learning. A Research Report.* Clevedon: Multilingual Matters, 1991. ISBN: 978–1853590894.

CANALE, M., SWAIN, M. 1980. Theoretical bases of communicative approaches to second language teaching and testing. *Applied Linguistics, 1,* 1–47. 1980.

CANALE, M., SWEIN, M. 1980. In: Knoch, U. 2009. *Diagnostic Writing Assessment: The Development and Validation of a Rating Scale.* Peter Lang Pub Inc. ISBN: 3631589816.

CARBONELL, B., M. 2004. *Museum studies: An Anthology of Context.* Blackwell Publishing Ltd. 2004. ISBN: 0631228306.

CHOMSKY, N. 1965. *Aspects of the theory of syntax*. Cambridge: M.I.T. Press. 1965. ISBN 9780262530071.

CIPRIANOVÁ, E. 2003. *Problémy integrácie kultúrneho obsahu do vyučovania angličtiny ako cudzieho jazyka a jeho vplyv na utváranie názorov a postojov študentov stredných škôl*. Dizertačná práca. Bratislava: UK. 2003.

CIPRIANOVÁ, E. 2008. *Kultúra a vyučovanie cudzieho jazyka*. Nitra: UKF, 2008. ISBN 978–80–8094–301–1.

COHEN, L., MANION, L., MORRISON, K.., 2007. *Research Methods in Education*. Routledge, 2007. ISBN: 9780415368780.

A Common European Framework of Reference for Language Learning, Teaching, Assesment. Council of Europe. 2001. [online]. [cit.19.3.2009]. Available on the internet: http://www.coe.int/t/dg4/linguistic/Source/Framework_EN.pdf. 2001.

CORBETT, J. 2003. *An Intercultural Approach to English Language Teaching*. Clevedon: Multilingual Matters, 2003. ISBN: 1853596833.

CROSSMAN, J., E. 2011. *Experiential Learning About Intercultural Communication Through Intercultural Communication. Internationalising a Business Communication Curriculum*. Journal of Intercultural Communication. ISSN 1404–1634, issue 25, March 2011. [online]. [cit. 12. 8. 2011]. Available on the internet: URL: http://www.immi.se/intercultural/.

CULLEN, B. 2000. *Practical Techniques for Teaching Culture in the EFL Classroom*. [online]. [cit. 20. 5. 2010]. Available on the internet: http://iteslj.org/Techniques/ Cullen-Culture.html. 2000.

CUSHNER, K., BRISLIN, R. 1997. *Improving Intercultural Interactions*. SAGE Publications, 1997. ISBN: 0761905375.

DAKOWSKA, M. 2007. *Teaching English as a Foreign Language*. Wydawnictwo Naukowe PWN. 2007. ISBN: 83–01–14498–2.

DAKOWSKA, M. 2004. *The Intercultural Aspects of CLIL*. Module einer bilingualen Didaktik und Methodik des Sachfachunterrichts. 2004. [online]. [cit.19.10.2009]. Available on the internet: *www.mobidic.org/doc/BI/ TheoriePraxisTexte/.../IntKultAspBilUnt-UK.pdf*.

DAMEN, L. 1987. Culture learning: The fifth dimension in the language class-room. Reading, MA: Addison-Wesley. 1987.

DEARDORFF, D., K. 2009. *The SAGE Handbook of Intercultural Competence*. Sage Publications. 2009. ISBN: 1412960452.

DOYÉ, P. (ed) 1991. *Grossbritannien. Seine Darstellung in deutschen Schulbüchern für den Englischunterricht*. Frankfurt: Moritz Diesterweg, 1991. ISBN: 978–3883042725.

DUNNETT, S., C., DUBIN, F., LEZBERG, A. 1986. English language teaching from an intercultural perspective. In Valdes, J., M. *Culture Bound*. Cambridge University Press, 1986. ISBN: 0521310458.

DUROCHER, D., O. 2007. Teaching Sensitivity to Cultural Difference in the First Year Foreign Language Classroom. *Foreign Language Annals*, Vol. 40, No. 1, p. 143–160. 2007.

EUROPUBLIC. 2007. *Languages and Cultures in Europe (LACE): The Intercultural Competences Developed in Compulsory Foreign Language Education in the European Union*. [online]. [cit. 9. 8. 2011] Available on the internet: ec.europa.eu/education/policies/lang/doc/lace_en.pdf. 2007.

FAERCH, C., HAASTRUP, K., PHILLIPSON, R. 1984. *Learner Language and Language Learning*. Clevendon: Multilingual Matters, 1984. ISBN: 978–0905028286.

FANTINI, A. E. 1995. Intercultural Interlocutor Competence Model. In: Deardoff, D., K. 2009. *The SAGE Handbook of Intercultural Competence*. Sage Publications. ISBN: 1412960452.

FANTINI, A.E. 2005. *About Intercultural Communicative Competence: A Construct*. [online]. [quoted 19th 8. 2010]. Available on the internet: www.sit. edu/SITOccasionalPapers/feil_appendix_e.pdf. 2005.

FANTINI, A. E., TIRMIZI, A. 2006. *Exploring and assessing intercultural competence*. Federation of the Experiment in International Living, Washington University. [online]. [quoted 2nd 8. 2011]. Available on the internet: http:// digitalcollections.sit.edu/cgi/viewcontent.cgi?article=1001&context=world-learning_publications&sei-redir=1#search=%22Exploring%20Assessing%20 Intercultural%20Competence%20ISBN%22

FLICK, U. 2009. *An introduction to Qualitative Research*. SAGE Publications. 2009. ISBN: 9781847873218.

FRIES, S. 2002. *Cultural, Multicultural, Cross-cultural, intercultural: A Moderators Proposal*. [online]. [cit.21.7.2010]. Available on the internet: www.tesol-france. org/articles/fries.pdf. 2002.

GAJDUŠEK, J. 2001. *Reálny a myšlienkový, experiment ako vyučovací prostriedok*. [online]. [cit.19.3.2009]. Available on the internet: http://kekule.science. upjs.sk/fyzika/didaktika/03.htm. 2001.

GALLOWAY, V.B. 1981. *Public Relations: Making an Impact*. In: Philips, J.K. and American Council on Teaching of Foreign Languages. Action for the '80s: A political, Professional, and Public Program for Foreign Language Education. National Textbook Company, Sokie. 1981.

GAVORA, P. 1998. Metóda verbálnych výpovedí v edukačnom výskume. In: *Metodológia vied o výchove*, Švec, Š. et al. Bratislava: IRIS, 1998. ISBN 80–88778–73–5.

GEERTZ, C. 1977. *The Interpretation of Cultures*. Basic Books, 1977. ISBN: 0465097197.

GILL, S., CANKOVA, M., MALEY, A. 2002. *Intercultural Activities*. Oxford Basics, 2002. ISBN: 9780194421782.

GÖBEL, K. 2007. *Qualität im interkulturellen Englischunterricht. Eine Videostudie*. Münster: Waxmann Verlag. 2007.

GRUSEC, J.E., HASTINGS, P.D. 2006. *Handbook of Socialization*, Guilford Press, 2006. ISBN: 1593853327.

GULLAHORN, J. T., GULLAHORN, J. E. 1963. An Extension of the U-Curve Hypothesis. In: Schein, R. 2008. *Landscape for a good citizen: The Peace Corps and the cultural logics of American cosmopolitanism*. Dissertation work. University of California.

GULLAHORN, J. T., GULLAHORN, J. E. 1963. An Extension of the U-Curve Hypothesis. *Journal of Social Issues*, 19, 3, 33–47, 1963. ISSN: 15404560.

GULLAHORN, J. T., GULLAHORN, J. E. 1963. An Extension of the U-Curve Hypothesis. In: Deardoff, D., K. 2009. *The SAGE Handbook of Intercultural Competence*. Sage Publications. 1963. ISBN: 1412960452.

HAGER, M. 2011. *Culture, Psychology, and Language Learning (Interkuclural Studies and Foreign Language Learning)*. Peter Lang Pub. Inc. 2011. ISBN: 978–3034301978.

HALLET, W. 1997. *The Bilingual Tiangle*: Überlegungen *zu einer Didaktik des bilingualen Sachfachunterichts*. Ministerium für Bildung, Wissenschaft and Weiterbildung, p. 6–15. 1997.

HAMMERLY, H. 1982. *Synthesis in language teaching*. Blaine, WA: Second Language Publications. 1982.

HARMER, J. 1991. *The Practice of English Language Teaching*. Longman ELT. 1991. ISBN: 0582046564.

HATCH, E.M. 1983. *Psycholinguistics: A second perspective*. Longman Higher Education, 1983. ISBN: 9780883772508.

HATCH, J., A. 2002. *Doing Qualitative Research in Education Settings*. State University of New York Press. 2002. ISBN: 0791455041.

HENDRICH, J. a kol. 1988. *Didaktika cizích jazyků*. Praha: Státní pedagogické nakladatelství, 1988.

HORVÁTHOVÁ, B. 2010. Significance of the Context in Translation of Idioms. In: *XLinguae.eu: A Trimestrial European Scientific Language Review*. Vol. 2, no. 2 (2010), p. 28–35. ISSN 1337–8384.

HORVÁTHOVÁ, B. 2013. Rozvoj integrovaného odborného a jazykového vyučovania (CLIL) a počítačom podporovaného vyučovania (CALL) pomocou vzdelávacích projektov. In: *Media4u Magazine*. Roč. 10, č. 3 (2013), s. 55–61. ISSN 1214–9187.

HORVÁTHOVÁ, B. 2013. Tracing the Development of Listening Strategies in the Absence of Explicit Instruction. In: *XLinguae: European Scientific Language Journal*. Vol. 6, no. 3 (2013), p. 32–41. ISSN 1337–8384.

HORVÁTHOVÁ, B. 2014. Implementing Language Learning Strategies into a Series of Second Foreign Language Learning Textbooks. In: *JoLaCE: Journal of Language and Cultural Education*. Vol. 2, no. 2 (2014), p. 60–94. ISSN 1339–4045.

HUGHES, G. 1986. An argument for cultural analysis in the second language classroom. In: Valdes, M. (ed.) *Cultural bound*. Cambridge University Press, 1986. ISBN: 0521310458.

HUHN, P. 1978. Landeskunde im Lehrbuch: Aspekte der Analyse, Kritik und korrektiven Behnadlung. In: Byram, M. 1989. *Cultural Studies in Foreign Language Education*. Multilingual Matters.

HYMES, D. 1972. On Communicative competence. In J.B.Pride and J.Holmes (eds) *Sociolinguistics*. Harmondsworth: Penguin, 1972. ISBN: 978–0140806656.

IMAHORI, T.T. – LANIGAN, L.M. 1989. Relational model of intercultural communication competence. In: *International Journal of Intercultural Relations*. Vol. 13, 1989, no. 3. 1989.

JOHNSON, K., JOHNSON, H. 1999. *Encyclopedic dictionary of applied linguistics: a handbook for language teaching*. Wiley-Blackwell. 1999. ISBN: 0631214828.

KING, P., BAXTER MAGOLDA, M., B. 2005. *A Developmental Model of Intercultural Maturity*. Journal of College Student Development. The Johns Hopkins University Press. 2005. ISSN: 08975264.

KING, P., BAXTER MAGOLDA, M., B. 2009. In: Deardoff, D., K. 2009. *The SAGE Handbook of Intercultural Competence*. Sage Publications. ISBN: 1412960452.

KNOCH, U. 2009. *Diagnostic Writing Assessment: The Development and Validation of a Rating Scale*. Peter Lang Pub Inc. 2009. ISBN: 3631589816.

KOLLÁRIK, T., SOLLÁROVÁ, E. 2004. *Metódy sociálnopsychologickej praxe*. Bratislava: Ikar, 2004. ISBN 80–551–0765–3.

KOSTKOVÁ, K. 2012. *Rozvoj interkulturní komunikační kompetence*. Brno: Masarykova univerzita. 2012. ISBN 978–80–210–6035–7.

KRAMSCH, C. 1993. *Context and Culture in Language Teaching*. Oxford: Oxford University Press, 1993. ISBN: 978–0194371872.

KRAMSCH, C. 1998. *Language and Culture*. Oxford: Oxford University Press, 1998. ISBN: 9780194372145.

KREY, K. *Content and Language Integrated learning (CLIL) and Introduction to Didactics and Methodology*. [online]. [cit. 9. 8. 2011]. Available on the internet: *www.eurocomi.net/booklet/booklet_CLIL_didacticsKatjaKrey.doc*.

LAKOFF, G., JOHNSON, M. 2003. *Metaphors We Live By*. University Of Chicago Press. 2003. ISBN: 978–0226468013.

LESSARD-CLOUSTON, M. 1997. Towards an Understanding of Culture in L2/FL Education. In: Ronko, K.G. *Studies in English*, 25, Japan: Kwansei Gakuin University Press. 1997.

LEVINE, D., R., ADELMAN, M., B. 1993. *Beyond language: cross-cultural communication*. Pearson Education. 1993. ISBN: 0130948551.

LINCOLN, Y., S., GUBA, E., G. 1985. *Naturalistic Inquiry*. Beverly Hills, Sage publications. 1985. ISBN: 978–0803924314.

LOVEDAY, L. 2003. Sociolinguistics of Learning and Using a Non-Native Language. In: Corbett, J. *An Intercultural Approach to English Language Teaching*. Multilingual Matters, 2003. ISBN: 1853596833.

LYSGAARD, S. 1955. Adaptation in a foreign society: Norwegian Fulbright guarantees visiting the United States. In: *International Social Science Bulletin*. Volume 7, p. 45–51. 1955.

MARTINEZ, A., G. 2002. Authentic Materials: An Overview on Karen's Linguistic Issues. [online]. [cit. 2. 8. 2010]. Available on the internet: http://www3.telus. net/linguisticsissues/authenticmaterials.html. 2002.

MARX, H. A. 2011. *Please Mind the Gap: A Pre-service Teacher's Intercultural Development During a Study Abroad Program*, BiblioBazaar, LLC. 2011. ISBN: 978–1243512475.

MONTECINOS, C., WILLIAMSON, G. 2010. Interculturalism, Multiculturalism and Diversity as Social and Educational Policies in Chile. In: Grant, C., A., Portera, A., *Intercultural and multicultural education: enhancing global inter-connectedness*. Routledge. 2010. ISBN: 978–0415876742.

MOON, D., G. 2007. Concepts of „Culture": Implications for Intercultural Communication Research. In: Asante, M., K., Miike, Y., Yin, J. *The Global Intercultural Communication Reader*. Routledge. 2007. ISBN: 978–0415958134.

NOVINGER, T. 2001. *Intercultural communication: a practical guide.* University of Texas Press. 2001. ISBN: 0292755716.

NUNAN, D., MILLER, L. 1995. *New Ways in Teaching Listening.* Alexandria, VA: Teachers of English to Speakers of Other Languages. 1995. ISBN: 0939791587.

NUTTALL, C. 1996. Teaching reading skills in a foreign language. London. Heinemann. 1996. ISBN: 1405080051.

PARMENTER, L. 2003. *Intercultural communicative competence.* [online]. [cit.19.8.2010]. Available on the internet: *tb.sanseido.co.jp/english/newcrown/pdf/ten001/ten_01_20.pdf.* 2003.

PELIKÁN, J. 1998. *Základy empirického výzkumu pedagogických jevů.* Praha: Karolinum, 1998. ISBN 80–7184–569–8.

POKRIVČÁKOVÁ, S. 2008. *CLIL plurilingvizmus a bilingválne vzdelávanie.* Nitra: ASPA, 2008. ISBN: 9788096964123.

POKRIVČÁKOVÁ, S., MENZLOVÁ, B., FARKAŠOVÁ, E. 2010. Creating Conditions for Effective Application of CLIL Methodology in Slovakia. In Silvia Pokrivcakova (ed.): *Modernization of Teaching Foreign Languages* (p. 7–20). Brno: Masaryk University. 2010. ISBN 978–80–210–5294–9.

POLE, Ch., J. 2003. *Ethnography for Education (Doing Qualitative Research in Educational Settings).* Open Univ Pr. 2003. ISBN: 978–0335206001.

PORTER, R. E., SAMOVAR, L. A. 1999. *Intercultural Communication: A Reader.* 9th edition. Belmont: Wadsworth Publishing Co Inc., 1999. ISBN: 978–0534562410.

POYATOS, F. 1992. Non-verbal communication in foreign language teaching: Theoretical and methodological perspectives. In A. Helbo (ed.) *Evaluation and Language Teaching.* Bern: Peter Lang. 1992. ISBN: 978–3261042835.

PRŮCHA, J. 1997. *Moderní pedagogika.* Praha: Portál. 1997. ISBN: 8071781703.

PRŮCHA, J. 2010. *Interkulturní komunikace.* Grada Publishing, 2010. ISBN: 9788024730691.

REID, E. 2009. Autentické materiály ako efektívna metóda jazykového vyučovania spojená s interkultúrnym porozumením. In Katerina Veselá (ed.) Cudzie jazyky v škole 6 (p. 90–94). Nitra: UKF. 2009. ISBN: 978–80–8094–549–7.

REID, E. 2010. Culture – an Inevitable Part of a Foreign Language Teaching. In Silvia Pokrivcakova (ed.) *Modernization of Teaching Foreign Languages* (p. 201–217). Brno: Masaryk University. 2010. ISBN: 978–80–210–5294–9.

REID, E. 2013. Models of Intercultural Competences in Practice. *International Journal of Language and Linguistics.* Vol. 1., No. 2, p. 44–53. 2013. ISSN: 2330–0221 (Online)

RICHARD, J.C. 2001. *Curriculum Development in Language Teaching.* Cambridge University Press. 2001. ISBN: 0521804914.

RICHARDS, J. C. 2001. *Curriculum Development in Language Teaching.* Cambridge University Press, 2001. ISBN: 0521804914.

ROBINSON, G. 1988. *Crosscultural understanding.* New York: Prentice-Hall. 1988.

Roshan Cultural Heritage Institute. Cultural understanding through education and communication. Definition of Culture. 2001. [online]. [cit.19.7.2010]. Available on the internet:http://www.roshan-institute.org/templates/System/details.asp?id=39783&PID=474552. 2001.

SAMOVAR, L.A., PORTER, R.E., McDANIEL, E.R. 2009. *Communication Between Cultures.* Wadsworth; International edition edition. 2009. ISBN: 0495567523.

SAMOVAR, L. A., PORTER, R. E., MCDANIEL, E. R. 2008. *Intercultural Communication:*
A Reader. Wadsworth. 2008. ISBN: 0495554219.

SEELYE, H. 1974. *Teaching culture: Strategies for foreign language educators.* Skokie, IL: National Textbook Company. 1974.

SERCU, L. 2000. *Acquiring Intercultural communicative competence from textbooks.* Leuven University Press, 2000. ISBN: 978–9058670267.

SERCU, L. 2005. *Foreign Language Teachers and Intercultural Competence.* Clevedon: Multilingual Matters, 2005. ISBN: 1853598437.

SERCU, L. 1995. *Intercultural Competence: Secondary School v. 1: A New Challenge for Language Teachers and Trainers in Europe (Language & Cultural Contact).* Aalborg Universitetsforlag: 1995. ISBN: 8773074977.

SILVERMAN, D. 2006. *Interpreting Qualitative Data.* London: Sage publications. 2006. ISBN: 978–1412922456.

SINGER, R.M. 1987. *Intercultural Communication: A Perceptual Approach.* Englewood Cliffs, New Jersey: Prentice Hall, Inc., 1987. ISBN: 978–0134691152.

Spoločný európsky referenčný rámec pre jazyky: učenie sa, vyučovanie, hodnotenie. 2001. [online]. [cit.19.3.2009]. Available on the internet: http://www.statpedu.sk/sk/filemanager#395. 2001.

SOENEN, R., VERLOT M., SUIJS, S. 1999. In: Dietz, G. 2009. *Multiculturalism, Interculturality and Diversity in Education: An Anthropological Approach.* Waxmann Verlag GmbH. 1999. ISBN: 978–3830921974.

SOROKIN, P. A. 1982. *Social and Cultural Dynamics.* Sargent (Porter), Publisher,U.S. 1982. ISBN: 978–0875580296.

STICKLER, U., EMKE, M. 2011. Literalia: Towards Developing Intercultural Maturity Online. *Language Learning & Technology*. Vol. 15, No. 1, p. 147–168. 2011.

STERN, H. H. 1993. *Issues and Options in Language Teaching*. Oxford: Oxford University Press, 1993. ISBN: 978–0194370660.

STRAUB, H. 1999. Designing a Cross-Cultural Course. English Forum, vol. 37: 3, July-September, 1999.

Štátny vzdelávací program pre 1. stupeň základnej školy v Slovenskej republike. Štátny pedagogický ústav. 2011. [online]. [cit. 18. 8. 2012]. Available on the internet: http://www.statpedu.sk/files/documents/svp/ 1stzs/isced1/vzdelava-cie_oblasti/anglicky_jazyk_isced1.pdf. 2011.

ŠVEC, Š et al. 1998. *Metodológia vied o výchove*. Bratislava: IRIS, 1998. ISBN: 8088778735.

THANASOULAS, D. 2001. *The Importance Of Teaching Culture In The Foreign Language Classroom*. In: Radical Pedagogy. 2001. ISSN: 1524–6345.

TITLEY, G. 2004. *Resituating Culture*. Council of Europe. 2004. ISNB: 9287153965.

TYLOR, E.D. 1920. *Primitive culture: researches into the Development of Mythology, Philosophy, Religion, Art, and Custom*. 2 volumes, London: John Murray, 1920 [online]. [cit.19. 7. 2010]. Available on the internet: http://on-linebooks.library.upenn.edu/webbin/book/lookupname?key=Tylor%2c%20 Edward%20Burnett%2c%20Sir%2c%201832–1917.

Učebné osnovy Anglický jazyk pre 1. – 4. ročník základnej školy. Jazykový vari-ant. Schválilo Ministerstvo školstva Slovenskej republiky dňa 20. septembra 2000 č. 3276/2000–41 s platnosťou od 1. septembra 2001. [online]. [cit.19. 3. 2009]. Available on the internet: http://www.statpedu.sk/Pedagogicke_doku-menty/Zakladne_skoly/Osnovy/UO_Aj_1–4.roc_jaz.doc. 2000.

Učebné osnovy Anglický jazyk pre 5. – 9. ročník základnej školy. Schválilo Ministerstvo školstva Slovenskej republiky dňa 27. septembra 1999 č. 3584/1999–41 s platnosťou od 1. septembra 2000. [online]. [cit. 19. 3. 2009]. Available on the internet: http://www.statpedu.sk/Pedagogicke_dokumenty/ Zakladne_skoly/Osnovy/UO_AJ_5.-9.roc.doc. 2000.

VALDES, J.,M. 1986. *Culture Bound*. Cambridge University Press, 1986. ISBN: 0521310458.

VAN EK, J.A. 1986. *Objectives for Foreign Language Learning, Vol.1: Scope*. Strasbourg: Council of Europe, 1986.

WARDHAUGH, R. 2009. *An Introduction to Sociolinguistics*. Oxford: Blackwell Publishers, 2009. 6th edition. ISBN: 978–1405186681.

WORF, B. 1956. *Language, Thought, and Reality: Selected Writings of Benjamin Lee Whorf.* MIT Press, 1956. ISBN: 978–0262730068.

ZARATE, G. 1990. The observation Diary: An Ethnographic Approach to Teacher Education. In: Buttjes, D., Byram, *M. Mediating Languages and Cultures: Towards an Intercultural Theory of Foreign Language Education.* Multilingual Matters. 1990. ISBN: 1853590711.

ZERZOVÁ, J. 2012. *Interkulturní komunikační kompetence a její rozvíjení v hodinách anglického jazyka na 2. Stupni ZŠ.* Brno: Masarykova univerzita. 2012. ISBN 978–80–210–5725–8.

Bibliographic note

The text of this publication includes parts of the following previously published articles:

REID, E. 2009. Autentické materiály ako efektívna metóda jazykového vyučovania spojená s interkultúrnym porozumením. In Katerina Veselá (ed.) Cudzie jazyky v škole 6 (p. 90–94). Nitra: UKF. 2009. ISBN: 978–80–8094–549–7.

REID, E. 2010. Culture – an Inevitable Part of a Foreign Language Teaching. In Silvia Pokrivcakova (ed.) *Modernization of Teaching Foreign Languages* (p. 201–217). Brno: Masaryk University. 2010. ISBN: 978–80–210–5294–9.

REID, E. 2012. Using TV Adverts in Intercultural Teaching. In: Pokrivčáková, S. *Cudzie jazyky a kultúry v* škole *9 = Foreign Languages and Cultures at School 9* (164–179). Nitra: UKF, 2012. - ISBN 978–80–558–0184–1.

REID, E. 2012. Compatibility of the National Curriculum in Slovakia with the CEFR with Respect to Intercultural Education. In: Horváthová, B. *New Directions in Teaching Foreign Languages* (138–157). Brno: Masarykova univerzita, 2012. - ISBN 978–80–210–6003–6.